DANCING WITH SALOMÉ
COURTING THE UNCANNY WITH
OSCAR WILDE AND FRIENDS

NINA ANTONIA

TRAPART*books*

Dancing with Salomé – Courting the Uncanny with Oscar Wilde and Friends

Trapart Books, 2021

Hardback ISBN 978-91-986920-2-0
Paperback ISBN 978-91-986920-0-6
E-book ISBN 978-91-986920-1-3

Trapart Books
P.O. Box 15
SE-598 21 Vimmerby
Sweden

info@trapart.net
www.trapart.net

Dancing with Salomé

'Taste, and remember all the summer days
That lie, like gold reflections in the lake
Of vanished years, unreal but sweet always;
Soft luminous shadows that I may not take
Into my hands again, but still discern
Drifting like gilded ghosts before my eyes,
Beneath the waters of forgotten things,
Sweet with faint memories,
And mellow with old loves that used to burn
Dead summer days ago, like fierce red kings...'

Lord Alfred Douglas
'Wine of Summer' August 1897

INTRODUCTION: A DARK MAGIC

The dark magic of the 1890s has been explored by historians, cultural theorists and literary scholars. The fin de siècle, also known as The Decadence, was an era with a peculiar, immediately recognisable style. It was mannered, sophisticated, polished and amoral. After the industrial revolution of the nineteenth century, and before the fast new beginning of the twentieth, the decadents stopped to rethink the arts, and to bring forward the powerful symbols of the unconscious mind. Their arts glorified their morbid tastes. They liked witty repartee, and disliked moralising. They appreciated costumes and artifice. They preferred the paradoxical to the obvious, moonlight to sunlight, and imagination to fact.

Among the throng of creative people during this era, sauntered Oscar Wilde. His career as a writer was distinguished, but the fame from that was eclipsed by the drama of his own life. He has become an icon of the fin de siècle. In this collection of essays by Nina Antonia we have the opportunity to appreciate Wilde in the context of the mystic, mythological and esoteric themes which flow through his works and were the well springs of his creativity.

In these essays, we see the minor and the major figures of fin de siècle London society, together, as they were at the time. Nina Antonia includes and illuminates the roles of marginal and forgotten characters, such as Lionel Johnson, and also explains the associations between Oscar Wilde's circle and seemingly unrelated characters such as Aleister Crowley.

I initially knew of the writings of Nina Antonia through her articles in the *Fortean Times* magazine. But I had no close acquaintance until a remarkable coincidence brought us together. Late in 2020, I was working on an article for *Hellebore* magazine, on the rumours that writing the novel *The Picture of Dorian Gray* had brought a malediction upon its author. At the very same time, Nina Antonia was writing an essay, (included here) published as 'A Purple Thread: The Supernatural Doom of Oscar Wilde.' The topic of Wilde and curses is not mainstream, and it was remarkable that the two of us, separately, were writing about it at the same time. Since then, I have read all her studies of the 1890s, and am honoured to write an introduction to this collection.

THE NOVEL

The Picture of Dorian Gray is itself a fluently written, richly descriptive, gothic novel, in which a cursed portrait reflects the true face of the increasingly debauched Dorian Gray. To read, or re-read the novel, immediately after reading Nina Antonia's collection of writings, makes one aware of how prescient it is. *Dorian Gray* is an allegory and a prophecy of the course of Oscar Wilde's own life. Almost every element of his fame and his downfall is to be found there, most especially in the statement about 'that pride of individualism that is half the fascination of sin.'

The essays in this volume explain much about the creator of this striking novel, and also its reception among Wilde's closest friends. As Nina Antonia points out, Lord Alfred Douglas, who so physically resembled the fictional Dorian Gray, read the novel many times before meeting Oscar Wilde. Douglas credited Wilde with an ability to cast a spell of glamour, by his use of words, and his description enhances our understanding of how Wilde lived and worked during his years at the pinnacle of London society.

I would suggest that the affinities between Dorian Gray and Lord Alfred Douglas went even further than the instances noted by Nina Antonia. Aside from the congruence of names, noted in 'How Shall Dead Men Sing,' there is the story of Dorian Gray's family. In the novel, the young man is an orphan, brought up by his grandfather, Lord Kelso, an old and loveless man, given to uncouth behaviour and episodes of rage. He is described as an 'English noble who was always quarrelling with the cabmen about their fares.' Dorian Gray remembered him with hatred.

It is easy to see the correspondence between this story, and that of the family of Lord Alfred Douglas, who detested his father, the Marquis of Queensberry, an eccentric whose violent behaviour often embarrassed his relatives. Queensberry's wife was able to divorce him, at a time when this was a difficult legal move, citing his cruelty as well as adultery. In order to succeed, her case must have presented evidence of an extreme type. Oscar Wilde was not acquainted with the Douglas family, and would not have known any of this, at the time that he wrote the novel. The echo of fact into fiction is astonishing.

FOREBODINGS

The above details show how a text can uncannily predict and echo events around its creator. Several writers, including myself, have explored the notion that *The Picture of Dorian Gray* was an occult novel, which reproduces some teachings of the Order of the Golden Dawn. This secret society was dedicated to ritual magic. Constance Wilde joined at the very time when her husband was writing *Dorian Gray*. The curses which the Golden Dawn put on initiates, as Nina Antonia explains here, bound them to secrecy, at risk of being slain by paralysis.

This was the fate suffered by Constance Wilde. She was the first of the series of people linked to Wilde and the infamous Queensbury trial who met an untimely death.

The notion that Oscar Wilde was under some sort of curse has been around for a long time, and perhaps started with Oscar himself. Nina Antonia has cited his statement that said that there was a "note of doom that like a purple thread" ran through his life.

The fatal combination of love, literature and obsession which bound Oscar Wilde to Lord Alfred Douglas is considered in this volume, with an explanation of the dark history of the aristocratic Douglas family.

One might add the history of the Wilde family to this picture. If Oscar Wilde was under a curse, it may not have simply been the work of the occultist circle that his wife joined, apparently with the aim of providing him inspiration for his fiction. The Wilde family had been haunted by repetitive events and inversions of success, for more than one generation.

In *The Trickster and the Paranormal* George P. Hansen, a scholar of the supernatural, has suggested that in all cultures there are manifestations an otherworldly, immortal force which is liminal, charismatic, unpredictable and destructive. Hansen terms this cross-cultural being the Trickster. Hansen suggests that people who engage with the paranormal, especially without any of the rituals or cultural protections which their national traditions might prescribe, tend to experience negative consequences. He points out that the characteristics of the Trickster – boundary crossing, deception, violation of sexual mores, and supernatural manifestations – tend to appear in the lives of people who have meddled with the paranormal, and usually lead to a decline in rational reasoning, disastrous decisions, and loss of status.

George P. Hansen does not assert the reality or otherwise of the Trickster, whom the monotheistic religions would equate with the demonic, and pagan religions with ambiguous entities such as the Native American Coyote spirit. His research leaves open the possibility that this dynamic force is a real, but incalculable part of the natural world in which we live. Or, it might be a projection of our own unconscious minds, which could have powers as yet unknown to us.

Oscar Wilde was proud of his family heritage. His mother was a poet and Irish nationalist, and his father a respected surgeon. Both were published writers. They were creative, privileged, outspoken people who lived with verve in the upper echelons of Irish society. Yet, in their later years, they had unexpected sorrows and reversals, and the pattern of their misfortunes was to be strangely prophetic of the life history of Oscar himself.

Lady Jane Wilde was active in seeking out and making a written record of Irish stories of the supernatural. She published a collection, *Ancient Legends, Mystic Charms and Superstitions of Ireland* in 1888. In many of the stories which she skilfully translated and transcribed, curses and uncanny events follow those who have offended spiritually powerful people, or the fairy inhabitants of the land.

It is evident that although both William and Jane Wilde were fascinated by Irish legends, they were not wary of the doom foretold for anyone who offended the immortal spirits. In 1864 they built a house on a significant heritage spot in County Sligo. As described here by Nina Antonia, 'the house stood on the site of a mythical battle between Danaan warriors from whom the Dana O'Shee are descended and the Fir-Bolg, contending for the magical lordship of Ireland.' Building on fairy lands is a proverbial way of attracting their ire.

The Wildes called the home, which they designed themselves, Moytura. It began as a splendid country seat, and the foundation of their family life. But their lives became stressed, after Dr William Wilde entered into a tempestuous relationship with Mary Travers, a young woman who had been his patient.

A discrete liaison between an older, privileged man and a young woman on a small income was the type of event which society allowed. Wives were supposed to look away if their husband had such an interest, and Lady Jane Wilde showed neither concern nor jealousy. But the relationship became passionate and obsessive, and Mary Travers would not be regulated to the side-lines of William Wilde's life. They had frequent quarrels and reconciliations, and the themes of love and hate in their correspondence, as Emer O'Sullivan writes in *The Fall of the House of Wilde*, 'is an uncanny foreshadowing, as we shall see, of Oscar's with Lord Alfred Douglas.' (O'Sullivan, 176)

In the mid 1860s Mary Travers began a campaign against Dr William Wilde, and hired post boys to distribute hostile pamphlets and lampoons during his public lectures. Exactly similar scenes were enacted by the Marquis of Queensberry, when he began a hateful pursuit of Oscar Wilde in London in the mid 1890s. The outcomes were similar, as Mary Travers and the Marquis of Queensbury were both involved in sensational libel suits, which destroyed reputations and attracted a voyeuristic public.

Dr William Wilde was not ruined and imprisoned, as his son Oscar was to be, but after the Mary Travers episode he was weakened in his health and social status. He retired and lived mainly at the country residence Moytura, amid the shades of the Celtic past. When he died, ten years later in 1876, his estate was found to be encumbered by debts. His family were dismayed, and astonished that all his wealth had evaporated. All of his extensive properties were mortgaged, and his wife was left nothing but the income from the land around their country house. Little could be earned from it, and Lady Wilde in her later years always referred to it as 'wretched Moytura.'

One of the tragedies of William Wilde's later years was the death of his two 'natural', that is to say, illegitimate daughters. These two sisters had been born in the years before his marriage. They were maintained in a respectable style and were known to his family. In 1871, on 31 October – All Hallows Eve – they attended a ball and suffered a tragic accident. Their crinoline dresses caught fire, and both died.

These losses would fit the expectations of any Irish person well versed in superstitions. The role of natural elements such as fire, and the significant date of 31 October, when magical forces are potent, are especially amenable to narratives about a supernatural curse. The events of later decades, when the repetition of obsessive love and hate brought doom on Oscar Wilde, also match occult schemas where the doubling of events is a sign of fate. The triple signifiers of boundary crossing, violation of sexual mores, and loss of status, are also evident. These are analysed by George P. Hansen as typical consequences of engagement with the paranormal.

If the house at Moytura did indeed bring ill-fortune to its owners, then the fall of the Wilde family could be added to Lady Wilde's volume of Celtic tales. However, there were other stories of tempting fate in this family.

In 1837 William Wilde, then a young graduate in medicine, made a journey to the Middle East, and was especially interested in the tombs and antiquities of Egypt. He collected many items, including pieces of a mummy which he used for scientific analysis. He also performed a remarkable feat, in climbing the Great Pyramid. This was extremely risky, as it involved a steep ascent, but he went all the way to the peak, and in one of those imperialistic gestures which so irritate Egyptians, carved his name into the stone. He then returned to Ireland, and began his career of initial successes, with a later toll of tragedy and failure.

Many Egyptian people would have told Dr Wilde, if they had been able to communicate with him, to respect the boundaries of the Great Pyramid, and do no such thing as climbing on it. Egyptian beliefs about maledictions and the strange significance of ancient sites are as potent as stories found in Ireland. Many people would have considered that William Wilde had brought a curse upon himself and his family. Exactly why he wanted to climb the Great Pyramid is unclear. It may simply have been his spirit of adventure. However, it is possible that the gesture had some ritual significance to him. Dr Wilde would have been a Freemason, and mystical theories about Pharaonic monuments were often found in lodge teachings during that era.

Whether or not one believes in synchronicities and omens of fate, one can identify remarkable patterns in the lives of the Wilde family. But supernatural explanations are not necessarily needed. An equally convincing explanation could be offered with reference to heredity and the decidedly material family curse of alcoholism. Addiction is inherited from one generation to the next. Like many Irish families, the Wildes had several members who died from the effects of alcohol – Oscar's older brother William among them. All of the family would have been affected by the irrational behaviours, and several disastrous decisions, such as Oscar Wilde's refusal to leave England when pursued by Queensberry, were made after drinking to excess.

The self-destruction of the addict is portrayed, in this volume, by Nina Antonia's sensitive and comprehensive account of the life of Lionel Johnson. Johnson's literary work and his lifestyle were both an intense display of the values of The Decadence. His mingling of religious themes and morbid disillusionment were typical of those who, like himself and Wilde, eventually converted to the Roman Catholic church. But even the Church could offer them salvation only in the next world. Doomed by the self-destructiveness of the addict, Lionel Johnson went into a decline. His talents, and his well-meaning friends, counted for nothing, for they could not save him from his dependence upon absinthe.

Nina Antonia's account of Lionel Johnson's last years is intriguing. While burdened with so many other problems, the poet took lodgings in a sinister haunted house. Was this an additional cause of his untimely death? Like a gothic novel, the lives of these Decadent literary figures provide both a natural and a supernatural explanation for their early deaths.

Historians rarely consider the influence of supernatural forces on the life of Oscar Wilde. The topic of curses and the occult are outside of rational narratives, although they are important to religious scholarship, anthropology and folklore studies. However, historians of the Decadence ought to give full representation of the distinctive ethos of the 1890s, an era when traditional religious and esoteric cult beliefs coexisted in artistic circles.

WILDE AND THE HISTORIANS

Throughout the whole of the twentieth century, as the fame of Oscar Wilde rose and rose again, biographers tended to take Wilde's own account of his misfortunes at face value. The dramatic and tragic tale set out in *De Profundis*, the famous prison letter, gives a devastatingly unsympathetic portrait of his romantic partner, Bosie. Although some commentators did not like the tone of recriminations in *De Profundis*, few were prepared to argue with its portrait of Wilde's doomed relationship.

This cannot be the whole story. The influence of literary executor Robbie Ross, with whom Wilde also had a volatile relationship, needs to be taken into account. Oscar Wilde's attempt to return to his relationship with Douglas, after his release from prison, is inexplicable if *De Profundis* is taken as a simple testimony of truth. In recent years, revisionist scholarship has suggested that the relationship between Wilde and his younger lover was a genuine romance, and one in which each offered something unique to the other. Nicholas Frankel, in *Oscar Wilde: The Unrepentant Years*, published in 2017, gives a sustained account of how Oscar Wilde's post prison life was not merely a miserable decline, but a time of self-definition and loyalty to his own nature. Nicolas Frankel explains the positive role which Douglas played in helping Wilde to write his later poetry.

In these essays, Nina Antonia provides a similar analysis, and gives an insightful review of both the lasting bonds between the two writers, as well as the inevitable decline of their passionate union. As well as offering an empathetic portrait of Lord Alfred Douglas, Nina Antonia shows the strange reflexive way that Oscar Wilde and Lord Alfred Douglas drew inspiration from each other, yet also were destructive of the very charisma which drew them together. The way that Bosie was both a blessing and a curse to Oscar Wilde makes fascinating reading, and it is in this volume that a reader will have the opportunity to integrate life studies, and the esoteric aspect of fin de siècle history, with its literary culture.

FAITH AND THE FUTURE

When lamenting his ruin, in *De Profundis*, Oscar Wilde knew that he had become a figure of infamy, while the people who trapped him into a lawsuit were public heroes. Wilde stated that the Marquis of Queensberry would be remembered as a hero of Sunday School tracts, while Bosie would be seen as an infant Samuel. Wilde supposed that he himself would sit in the circles of the infernal realm, somewhere between Gilles de Retz and the Marquis de Sade.

Although Oscar Wilde wrote this with bitterness, his sentiments were due to his regret that the Marquis of Queensberry had triumphed over him, and also his regret that his tarnished love, Bosie, appeared so innocent in the public eye. Ultimately, however, Wilde would not mind too much that he had been placed alongside such sinister and controversial figures. Sade and Gilles de Retz were both regarded with fascination by the French symbolists and decadents. They were transgressive and powerful. Although he was a Christian, and very much a man of faith, Wilde detested Sunday School tracts and piety. He returned to the topic later on in *De Profundis* and commented that the villain of medievalism, and the author of *Justine*, would 'prove better company' than the people who admired Queensberry, who was 'an ape and a buffoon.'

This reasoning appears significant to me. Oscar Wilde wanted to save his family name from the indignity of his prison sentence. But he did not want the admiration of trite moralists, and he never broke with the dark, shimmering, imaginative world of the 1890s artists. Oscar Wilde maintained his faith in Christ, but, as he explained in *De Profundis*, he knew Jesus to be the ultimate individualist whose life was a poem, and whose gift to humanity is the romance of art, kindled whenever creative beings make beautiful texts and images.

Oscar Wilde's life was filled with uncanny themes – precognition in his creative works, doomed patterns in his relationships, and a sense of destiny. These patterns are wonderfully explored by Nina Antonia, who gives equal attention to the light and shade which produced his dramatic and gothic fiction, *The Picture of Dorian Gray*.

– Therese Taylor, PhD, Author of *Bernadette of Lourdes, Her Life, Death and Visions* (Bloomsbury, London 2008).

REFERENCES

❧ Nicholas Frankel, *Oscar Wilde: The Unrepentant Years*, Harvard University Press, 2017.

❧ George P Hansen, *The Trickster and the Paranormal*, Xlibris, Corp., 2001

❧ Emer O'Sullivan, *The Fall of the House of Wilde: Oscar Wilde and His Family*, Bloomsbury 2006

❧ Therese Taylor, 'The Curse of Dorian Gray,' *Hellebore*, No 3, 31 Oct 2020, p 37-43

❧ Oscar Wilde, *De Profundis and Other Writings*, Penguin Books, London 1987

DANCING WITH SALOMÉ: AN INTRODUCTION

There are certain subjects that prove irresistible to biographers; Oscar Wilde especially so. Few lives are quite as tumultuous as Wilde's. He rode the rapids from triumph to ruination with barely a breath in-between. Although statuesque & stylish, the Dublin born playwright was not traditionally handsome, a deficit that he was more than able to make up for with an innate glamour. A term that has its origins in magic, to 'throw glamour' is to create a powerful, enticing, illusion or, as Scott notes in *The Lay of the Last Minstrel*: Glamour could make 'a lady seem a knight' or 'the cobwebs on a dungeon wall seem tapestry in lordly hall.' An enchanting story teller with a mellifluous voice, Oscar cast a spell few could resist as his 'homme fatale' 'Bosie', real name, Lord Alfred Douglas, would later admit. Oscar Wilde's craft was words, with which he could beguile, seduce, influence and amuse. Whether spoken or written, these words carried as if on wings, their tips silvered in charm. However, it was also words, in a love letter to Lord Alfred Douglas, which would be Wilde's undoing. Oscar's parents, both eminent folklorists steeped in Celtic knowledge gave their youngest son a childhood in which the supernatural was very much alive. There is no imagination as powerful as that of a child, particularly one as gifted as Oscar Wilde, and he nurtured that wonder into a graceful and privileged adulthood.

Not only was Oscar Wilde superstitious; he regularly consulted palm readers and fortune tellers. Though sophisticated, he was not a cynic and his work is abundant with the uncanny, which ultimately came to be reflected in his life. In *De Profundis,* the scathing prison letter written to Lord Alfred Douglas, Wilde speaks of 'Bosie's' accursed bloodline but he does not recognise his own, even though he claimed to have been visited by the ghost of his mother, 'Speranza', on the eve of her death. Such a vision is known as a 'crisis apparition' and often carries a warning, although Oscar might well have concluded that the worst had already happened. Many excellent authors, including

Matthew Sturgis, the latest in a long line to tackle a Wilde biography, pay little heed to the supernatural aspects of Oscar's life and work. Folklore as an academic subject is gaining acceptance but the supernatural remains unquantifiable. The stability of W.B Yeats, a member of numerous occult societies, is unusual, though he tended towards the mystical rather than the occult, unlike Aleister Crowley. Perhaps it is a matter of goals, for Yeats was a seeker of knowledge whilst Crowley sought power and the appeasement of his immense, wildfire ego that consumed all in his path. In his pursuit of infamy, the self-proclaimed 'Great Beast' stalked Lord Alfred Douglas via literary means, hoping to lure him into a public court battle. Impetuous though he was, Douglas knew better than to enter into unseemly litigation with one such as Aleister Crowley.

Men of great passions leave legacies of flame. Oscar Wilde died as a pariah and rose like a phoenix, a process which has led to the character assassination of Lord Alfred Douglas. In a society where scope of vision is ever narrowing and nuance is a lost art, polarities become increasingly extreme as John D. Stratford, who manages the estate of Lord Alfred Douglas concurs: 'Lord Alfred Douglas has seldom fared well in biographies of Wilde, starting with Ransome in 1912 and especially Frank Harris in 1916. However, while he was alive, he was able to defend himself and often did in the Law Courts winning thousands in damages. With his death in 1945 all libel restraints were removed. The first major biography of Wilde after 1945 was by Hesketh Pearson who treated Bosie well as he had the opportunity to discuss the story with many people who knew Wilde, including Bosie. Elmann's magnificent biography of Wilde in 1987 unfortunately includes a few unnecessarily spiteful and inaccurate comments about Bosie but is nowhere as bad as some of those that followed. The main attacks on Bosie tend to centre around the myths that he 'forced' Wilde to take the action against his father and that he 'abandoned' Wilde in Naples. The facts show both to be false, however, as Oscar said, "The truth is rarely pure and never simple."

The key to this interlinking portmanteau of essays is to be found in Vincent O'Sullivan's book *Aspects of Wilde* (1938) which deserves a reprint though it would challenge modern readers used to the current representation of Wilde, claiming as it does that no one forced Oscar to do anything he didn't want to do. O'Sullivan, who was friends with both Oscar and Bosie, comments in his slender but telling tome that Aubrey Beardsley and others in his circle believed it unlucky to have any of the playwright's books in the house. *Aspects* is possessed of an ominous foreboding, the old lady that Oscar says they mustn't look at because she is a witch, the ghosts of suicides that dwell in an Italian garden. It is a haunted book but then Vincent O'Sullivan, like Wilde, was Irish and of the generation of writers that were more open to the unseen. Sadly, it is also true that many of Oscar Wilde's family and companions were ill-fated: Constance, his wife, died in agony; 'Speranza,' once so proud of her youngest son, appeared as a death-mask of her former self, bowed by sorrow before her demise. Ironically, it was Oscar's mother who pressed him to fight in court and clear the name of Wilde. Friends too fell like so many leaves from an autumn tree, not least Vincent O'Sullivan, the scion of a once prosperous family suffered the ignominy of a pauper's grave. The poet Lionel Johnson, the catalyst who introduced Lord Alfred to Oscar Wilde, drank himself to death whilst being menaced by a fearsome avian entity and Bosie Douglas was condemned to a long life in which his 'red rose leaf lips' withered and his blonde hair faded to frost, a witness to the destruction of all he had held dear.

A PURPLE THREAD
– THE SUPERNATURAL DOOM OF OSCAR WILDE

'Common sense is the enemy of romance,' wrote Oscar Wilde in response to an invitation to join the 13 Club, a London society that sought to debunk superstition; 'Leave us some unreality.' Indeed, to write of Wilde whilst neglecting enchantment would be like excluding one of the colours of the rainbow. The supernatural threaded its influence, invisible yet undeniable, throughout the life and work of Oscar Wilde, and he embraced it with his entire being. A mystical Irish bard for the modern age, Wilde made magic with words. As his homme fatale, Lord Alfred Douglas, was to concur in his autobiography, 'Oscar did succeed in weaving spells. One sat and listened to him enthralled. It was indeed enchantment and nothing else.' But many a magical being has stumbled into a snare, and Wilde later acknowledged that his craft had forced the hand of fate: 'Words! Mere words! How terrible they were! What a subtle magic there was in them. They seemed to be able to give a plastic form to formless things.'

Both Oscar's father William and his mother Lady Jane Francesca – whose poetry was published under the name 'Speranza' – were eloquent dream-weavers, continuing the Gaelic tradition of storytelling while collecting and publishing their own anthologies of Irish folklore. It's no surprise, then, that Oscar's childhood was abundant with myth and legend. Born on October 16th, 1854, and baptised Oscar Fingal O'Flahertie Wills Wilde, his extravagant moniker reflected his parent's love of folklore. Fingal, a mighty warrior king and bard, hailed from James Macpherson's popular eighteenth-century Ossian poems. In them, Fingal's son Ossian, himself a poet, ventures to Tír na nÓg, land of eternal youth, where he and the golden-haired fairy princess Niamh sire a magical child they name Oscar.

The supernatural wasn't just to be found in the literature of young Oscar's life, but in the very landscape. William Wil-

'I myself would sacrifice everything for a new experience.'

de chose a country house for his family in Moytura, County Sligo, itself believed to be the fabled Tír na nÓg, populated by the heroic fairies of Ireland, the Dana O'Shee. Some say these beings are fallen angels who were too good for hell. Dwelling under magical rocks and in fairy glens, the Dana O'Shee come out to play on Beltane and caper with spirits at Samhain. The Wildes would have appeased them with a customary saucer of milk, for the house stood on the site of a mythical battle between Danaan warriors from whom the Dana O'Shee are descended and the Fir-Bolg, contending for the magical lordship of Ireland. The opposing sides met on Midsummer Day, the people of the Goddess Danu appearing as a flaming line holding aloft scarlet shields to protect themselves against their enemies' glittering spears. William Wilde wrote extensively about the battle and the area in his book *Lough Corrib, Its Shores and Islands*, and would take Oscar walking amongst the strange crags which are believed to be relics of the great battle. In *Ancient Legends, Mystic Charms, and Superstitions of Ireland*, Speranza noted, 'The mythology of a people reveals their relation to a spiritual and invisible world.' Although in later life Oscar's romantic visions transferred to Greece, Italy, and Arcady's fauns, nymphs, and fey, he remained a Celtic bard at heart, a son of star-dappled, spirit haunted violet twilights, able to connect the landscape with ancient legend wherever he roamed.

Wilde's charming, if somewhat theatrical, aspect was inherited from his mother and nurtured by the company kept by their family. A statuesque and grandiose woman who weaved mystical mistletoe into her dark brown hair, Speranza must have seemed a pagan goddess to her spellbound son. As well as compiling Irish lore, she also translated Wilhelm Meinhold's racy gothic novel *Sidonia the Sorceress* from German to English. Based on a true story, the lowly yet beautiful Sidonia corrupts and charms her way through umpteen priests and noblemen, participating in all manner of devilish cavorts before a cruel dispatch. Sidonia's dark glamour was to loom large in Wilde's imagination, as did that of another gothic figure, Melmoth the Wanderer, the creation of Oscar's great-uncle Charles Maturin. A seventeenth-century gentleman of Anglo-Irish descent, Melmoth sells his soul to the Devil for 150 years of pleasure, during which time he searches the world over for someone to lift the pact from him. Maturin's book concludes with a relative destroying an image of the damned Melmoth. The celebrated author of supernatural fiction, Joseph Sheridan Le Fanu, attended Lady Wilde's Saturday salons in Dublin's Merrion Square. Years later, Le Fanu would perish from an overdose of laudanum he took to combat nightmares of being buried alive, but his seductive vampire Carmilla was to become one of horror's eternals. In this creative domain of darkness and delight, the literary and the mystical overlapping in the most tragic of ways, it is easy to see the first flickerings of Dorian Gray, a shadow cast by candlelight.

❦

As a child, Oscar claimed to have heard the banshees' ominous keening foretelling the death of a relative. An ability to hear the Bean-Sidhe's cry is both a blessing and curse, as Lady Wilde explains in *Ancient Legends*: 'Music and poetry are fairy gifts, and the possessors of them show kinship to the spirit race—therefore they are watched over by the spirit of life, which is prophecy and inspiration; and by the spirit of doom, which is the revealer of the secrets of death.' Tragically, Oscar's beloved younger sister, Isola, was to perish from a brain fever in her tenth year. Isola's death shattered the Wilde household. If Speranza's musings held any weight, the child's passing into the shadow realm would have strengthened Oscar's kinship with the world of spirit, though it did nothing to expunge his grief. Literature however, did offer a form of immortality. After finishing Oxford University with a first in 1878, Wilde sought to make his way as a poet and playwright.

It wasn't until he became a father that he began exploring the enchanted realm of childhood themes. However, as exquisite as his fairy tales 'The Happy Prince,' 'The Selfish Giant,' and 'The Star Child' may be, at heart they are redemption parables written for his young sons, Cyril and Vyvyan. Two of Oscar's other short stories, 'Lord Arthur Savile's Crime' and 'The Canterville Ghost' have all the ingredients of horror, including murder and betrayal, but curiously lack sinister intent. Horror must take a razor to sentimentality. Significantly, when Dorian Gray kills the artist Basil Hallward in his old nursery, he is making a symbolic severance from childhood. *The Picture of Dorian Gray* was initially published in *Lippincott's Magazine* in June 1890, a revised and extended version released as a novel the following April. As Oscar stated in *De Profundis*, 'Every single work of art is the fulfilment of a prophecy,' but none more so than Dorian Gray, which was to wreak havoc not only on the life of its creator but on those closest to Wilde as well, including his wife, Constance, whom he had married in 1884.

A poignant cameo of Oscar and Constance's life together occurred in the early years of their marriage. Both had a predilection for aesthetic finery and, whilst enjoying a stroll, they caught the attention of a lippy urchin who proclaimed: 'Amlet and Ophelia out for a walk,' to which Oscar responded, 'My little fellow, you are quite right.' Sadly a bit too right, as their union was destined to be a tragic one.

As her husband made ready to write *Dorian Gray*, Constance pledged herself to the newly established Hermetic Order of the Golden Dawn, taking her vows on November 13, 1888. With this, she joined one of the most influential occult groups of the nineteenth century. The Golden Dawn boasted a lambent membership that at different times included W. B. Yeats, Algernon Blackwood, Arthur Machen, Florence Farr, Dion Fortune, and Aleister Crowley. As with all esoteric orders, there was a penalty for breaking the Golden Dawn's vows of secrecy, which includes being 'slain or paralysed without visible weapon, as if blasted by the Lightning Flash!' as Constance's biographer, John Murray notes in *The Tragic and Scandalous Life of Mrs. Oscar Wilde*. Murray posits that Constance discussed the rituals of the Hermetic Order with Oscar as he was bringing Dorian Gray to life. Wilde, who had joined the Masonic Apollo University Lodge whilst at Oxford, would have known that discretion is essential when participating in a closed order. Constance remained with the Golden Dawn for at least a year, attaining the level of Senior Philosopher. She also maintained an interest in the Theosophical Society and, with her husband, consulted the popular oracle Mrs. Robinson, whom Oscar dubbed 'the Sybil of Mortimer Street.'

The Wildes appeared to be the very picture of a fashionable couple dwelling within an artistic milieu. Oscar had also begun a relationship with the art critic Robbie Ross, but the elaborate framework of all their lives still held until the publication of *The Picture of Dorian Gray*. 'It seems as if Oscar had,' wrote Philippe Jullian in his biography of Wilde, 'a premonition of his own ruin, inevitable although delayed by success, in the way he shows Dorian's beauty suddenly crumbling into decay. The clash between the life he led, his material pleasures, and the life he dreamed of, could only lead to catastrophe.'

Reactions to the book were not all favourable, the conservative retailer W. H. Smith & Son refusing to stock it, whilst an anonymous review in the *Daily Chronicle* declared the novel, 'a tale spawned from the leprous literature of the French Décadents.' No one could have been more eloquent than Oscar in Dorian's defence: 'What is termed sin is an essential element of progress.' The sorcerer's spell finally manifested in June 1891, when the poet Lionel Johnson introduced Oscar Wilde to a delectable nineteen-year-old, Lord Alfred Douglas. It was as if the novelist's own fatally alluring creation, Dorian Gray, had taken form. Constance's biographer Joyce Bentley described Lord Alfred Douglas as 'a beautiful and disobedient angel,' if willful angels possess hair like spun gold, sapphire blue-eyes, and radiant alabaster complexions. Yet for all his beauty, Lord Alfred was like Dorian Gray—an ill-starred portent. The aristocratic Douglas hailed from a doomed, eldritch bloodline, 'where ruin followed like the echo of a bitter cry,' as Oscar was to later comment in *De Profundis*, his scourging prison letter to Lord Alfred.

Needless to say, it was Dorian Gray who really brought Wilde and Lord Alfred together, the young aristocrat becoming enraptured by the book after he was given a copy by Johnson, a university pal who was already acquainted with Oscar. History was made in the blink of a sapphire blue eye on the day the two young men jumped into a hansom cab and visited Wilde in his plush Chelsea home. Lord Alfred would later decry *The Picture of Dorian Gray* as 'an agent of magic and a tool for seduction,' but Wilde's novel has seduced us all and is now regarded as a classic work of the supernatural, inspiring countless reprints, numerous films, and even an opera. The premise of the tale—the separation of a man from his soul—is not an original one, as Oscar himself admitted, but it is one of the most bejewelled and compelling of descents. Furthermore, the book's allusions to homosexuality as the aristocratic Dorian is seduced by the decadent doctrines of a Faustian older man, Lord Henry Wotton, are unflinchingly brave. (Homosexuality had been criminalised under the punitive 1885 Criminal Law Amendment Act; after its passage the law was known as 'the blackmailer's charter.') A dabbler in the mystic arts, Dorian stands on a precipice, uncertain as to whether to join a 'Catholic community' or proffer his soul to stay as eternally beautiful as his portrait. Vanity triumphs, but the book is ultimately a tragedy, Gray imbibed like a fatal yet irresistible poison by men and women alike.

Just as Oscar's childhood sprang from the pages of a book, so it would seem that fate had written Lord Alfred Douglas into his life. Lord Alfred hailed from Scotland's oldest and most feared family, their ascendancy to wealth, land, and title steeped in the blood of their enemies. Their battle cry did indeed bring ruin, the very mention of the Douglas name—a Celtic derivation of 'dark grey'—dread. History first records them in the eighth century, when an overthrown lord asked to know the name of the victor. A soldier responded Sholto Douglas—'behold the dark grey man.'

The Douglas chieftains liked to preface their names with a suggestion of character; thus there was The Black Douglas and The Grim Douglas, not to mention a Dull Douglas and even a murderous Bell–the-Cat Douglas. Lord Alfred continued the tradition, using the charming soubriquet 'Bosie,' a derivative of 'Boysie' bestowed upon him by his doting mother Sybil. Life had denied Bosie nothing except a good father and a stable lineage; few of the Douglas men had gone quietly into eternity. Several were killed in battle, others perished in captivity. Fatal duels were commonplace and death by aggrieved relatives not unheard of. Whether by accident or design, there was a shockingly high quotient of firearm fatalities, whilst suicide was alarmingly prevalent and at least one fatality was attributed to sorcery. Or as Oscar was to summarise in *De Profundis*, 'You had yourself often told me how many of your race there had been who had stained their hands in their own blood; your uncle certainly, your grandfather possibly; and many others in the mad, bad line from which you come.' A bloody summation, not just suggestive of Dorian Gray but Lord Arthur Savile, who, following the murder of a palm-reader, imagines 'he could detect the stain of blood already upon his hands.'

Rumours of a Douglas family curse lurked in the endless corridors of their Scottish estate, Kinmount, a vast gloomy mansion set in 30,000 acres of land. The property would be sold off to pay for the accrued gambling debts and mistress upkeep of Bosie's irascible, negligent father, John Sholto Douglas, the Ninth Marquess of Queensberry.

Although Oscar was not Bosie's usual type, his taste running to younger men, Lord Alfred was enchanted by Wilde's poetical visions, saying of Oscar, 'He viewed everything from an unexpected angle; he clothed the most insignificant objects with beauty, wonder, terror; where others saw oranges he beheld gold.' (*Mercure De France*, 1895) Thus their mutual attraction to male prostitutes was for Wilde a magnificent adventure which he called 'feasting with panthers.' During this period, Oscar began sporting an Egyptian-style scarab ring. A popular talisman, the scarab symbolises creation and resurrection, and for Wilde an omen. Had he but known it, Oscar was to lead two very separate lives: before Dorian Gray and after. In April 1893, whilst his play 'A Woman of No Importance' was enjoying a successful run at the Haymarket Theatre in the West End, Oscar attended a party to which the famed palmist Cheiro had also been invited. Those who wished to have their palms read slipped their hands through a curtain so that Cheiro would not know to whom they belonged. Oscar's left hand was one assured of success, but the right was that, the palmist declared, 'of a king who would send himself into exile.'

'At what date?' Wilde anxiously enquired.

'A few years from now.'

❧

Oscar's exile – at least from his home life – had already commenced, with residences in hotels ostensibly to work but also to play as his relationship with Lord Alfred Douglas intensified. Callously, Wilde wrote to his former lover, Robbie Ross, exclaiming of Bosie 'he lies like a hyacinth on the sofa and I worship him.' Robbie, always so loyal to Oscar, now found himself, like Constance Wilde, delegated in Wilde's affections. Lyrically effusive, Oscar lavished Bosie with the rose-petals of his imagination, often by post. Unfortunately, seventeen-year-old Alfred

Wood obtained some of these letters after Douglas gave him a suit in which he had foolishly kept them. Although Wood had been treated generously by both Lord Alfred and Oscar Wilde, who had shared his affections, he showed up at the Haymarket Theatre clutching a sheaf of the very bankable love notes to blackmail the playwright. Despite Wilde handing over enough money to ensure that Mr. Wood enjoyed a year-long respite in America, one of Oscar's missives to Bosie got into general circulation: 'My Own Boy, your sonnet is quite lovely, and it is a marvel that those red rose-leaf lips of yours should be made no less for the madness of music and song than for the madness of kissing. Your slim gilt soul walks between passion and poetry. I know Hyacinthus, whom Apollo loved so madly, was you in Greek days.' It would circulate until the cruel day it fell into the clutches of Bosie's father, upon whom Wilde bestowed the title of 'The Screaming Scarlet Marquess.'

As the newly erected statue of Eros in Piccadilly shot arrows into lovers' hearts, Oscar Wilde soaked up ovations across theatre-land. He was, however, becoming haughty. Blinded by the glitter of his own brilliance, the actors in his celebrated plays no longer appeared to him as performers but puppets who danced to his words, yet Wilde, like Lord Alfred Douglas, was also a marionette, dancing to 'the note of doom that like a purple thread runs through the texture of Dorian Gray,' as he wrote in *De Profundis*. Here Wilde plucks at a refrain reminiscent of his mother's comments on 'unseen agencies,' telling in her *Ancient Legends* how 'people live habitually under the shadow and dread of invisible powers.' It was a theme to which Oscar would return.

Meanwhile Bosie, even more distracted than usual, dropped out of Oxford University, much to his parents' dismay. Lord Alfred's last notable act before his departure from university was a review of Wilde's play *Salomé* for the magazine he edited, *The Spirit Lamp*. Oscar, who had written the play in French, subsequently asked Bosie to translate it. How many times can one tempt fate? Like *The Picture of Dorian Gray*, Wilde's *Salomé* is steeped in ill-omen, not least the death of the captain of the guard. His death is announced by the page: 'He was my brother and nearer to me than a brother,' a minor comment but one that was to prove horribly prophetic. In bitter hindsight, Wilde later conferred the judgement of Salomé upon Bosie: 'I discern in all our relations not Destiny merely but Doom: Doom because she goes to the shedding of blood. Through your father you come of a race, marriage to whom is horrible, friendship fatal, and that lays violent hands either on its own life, or on the lives of others.'

Despite a good income, Oscar was struggling to support both a family and Bosie, whilst the lovers argued over *Salomé*, Wilde pointing out 'the schoolboy faults' of the translation. Concerned about Bosie's increasingly erratic behaviour, Oscar wrote to Lord Alfred's mother, Lady Queensberry, with whom he was on polite terms: 'Bosie seems to me to be in a very bad state of health. He is sleepless, nervous, and rather hysterical. He seems to me quite altered . . . he does absolutely nothing, and is quite astray in life.' Lady Queensberry hardly needed an excuse, and subsequently arranged for Lord Alfred to go to Egypt for a vacation that she hoped would culminate in his taking up a diplomatic post. But Bosie was a hedonistic playboy, as changeable as the moon's reflection on the Nile. Whilst in Egypt, he responded to a letter from his mother, in which she lamented that Wilde had 'the part of a Lord Henry Wotton' and was murdering her son's soul. Kindly but firmly, Bosie refuted Sybil's allegations: '*Dorian Gray* is a book of exaggerated types, it is all supernatural and unreal. Nobody wants to murder anyone else's soul. The whole idea and your whole attitude is really morbid and hysterical.' Despite the *Salomé* rift and Sybil's hopes that Bosie—the least diplomatic of all creatures—might settle in Egypt, he and Wilde reunited in Paris and returned to London an item. Douglas remained passionately attached to Wilde, whilst Oscar could not resist his 'gay, gilt, and gracious lad' especially when he was contrite. But 'the naked, fleshless feet of the spirit' as Lady Wilde described the otherworldly, still held sway upon Oscar. He revisited the Sybil of Mortimer Street, Mrs. Robinson, who exclaimed to him ominously, 'I see a very brilliant life for you up to a certain point. Then I see a wall. Beyond the wall I see nothing.'

Mrs Robinson's prediction echoed that of Cheiro's a year earlier, but the note of dread had not yet been struck until the entrance of the Screaming Scarlet Marquess on April 1, 1894. Lord Alfred and Oscar had been dining at the Café Royal when the Marquess had sidled over to their table and partaken of their wine. The afternoon passed well enough, only for Bosie to receive a vile epistle from his father, demanding that he end relations with Oscar. Signing off, 'Your disgusted so-called father,' Queensberry also threatened to shoot Wilde. Sadly, this was not untypical, the Marquess having recently unleashed a similar campaign of intimidation against the foreign secretary, Lord Rosebery, who was ensconced in a relationship with Bosie's older brother, Francis, Viscount Drumlanrig.

Unlike Francis, a retiring soul who shied from controversy, Bosie fired off a furious if brief telegraph, the contents of which were to become infamous: 'What a funny little man you are.' Now officially at war with his father, Lord Alfred purchased a gun and a sword-stick for Oscar, a change from the usual jewellery. In June 1894, the Marquess, with a prize-fighter in tow, forced his way into Wilde's home. Despite his florid manner, the playwright was not a man to be toyed with, and he stood up to a torrent of allegations including Queensberry's 'I hear you were thoroughly well blackmailed for a disgusting letter you wrote to my son.' Quick as ever, Wilde retorted, 'I never write except for publication.' The episode appeared to come to a noisy conclusion when Bosie accidentally fired his pistol through the ceiling of the Berkeley hotel. But it was merely a precursor to yet another Queensberry tragedy—the death of Francis, Viscount Drumlanrig, on October 18, whilst out hunting. Like his grandfather thirty-five years earlier, Drumlanrig, a man with military service, died 'accidentally' from a gunshot discharged in the mouth. Rumours persisted that Francis was being blackmailed for his affair with Lord Rosebery, the newly elected prime minister, and had committed suicide. At the time of Drumlanrig's death, Wilde and Bosie had been going through one of their lulls, the playwright driven to distraction by the gilt boy's demands on his time and pocketbook. Yet it was Oscar who gave Bosie flowers to place on his brother's grave. It was also Oscar who had prophesied Drumlanrig's cruel fate in the opening scenes of *Salomé*, amidst a descriptive abundance of red roses symbolising spilled blood.

The veracity of the Queensberry curse was now achingly apparent. 'I need not go further into more instances of the strange doom you seem to have brought on me in all things big or little,' Oscar would come to ponder in his cell. 'It makes me feel sometimes as if you yourself had been merely a puppet worked by some secret and unseen hand to bring terrible events to a terrible issue.' Again, Wilde sought out the Sybil of Mortimer Street. This time the news was more uplifting, Mrs. Robinson predicting a 'nice long journey' for Oscar. The playwright assumed it was the vacation to Algiers he was planning to take with Bosie. Even abroad, however, Wilde could not shake off a feeling of unease. He returned to London in time for the opening night of his latest play, *The Importance of Being Earnest*, on February 14, 1895. Banned from entering the theatre, the Screaming Marquess deposited a bouquet of vegetables at the stage door. Queensberry was relentless in his pursuit of the playwright, stalking him from theatre to restaurant to club, Wilde declaiming the sinister affect as 'the shadow that hunts with the beast of prey.' On February 18, Queensberry left a card for Wilde at the Albermarle Club, accusing him of 'posing as a Somdomite [sic].' Oscar expressed his alarm in a note to Robbie Ross: 'I don't see anything now but a criminal prosecution. My whole life seems ruined by this man. The tower of ivory is assailed by the foul thing.' Mrs. Robinson, however, predicted that Wilde would 'triumph.' Unfortunately, clairvoyance is an ephemeral art. Oscar did indeed triumph, as a renowned literary figure and a martyr for change, but not until after his untimely death.

Wilde felt that he had no choice but to act, charging the Marquess with libel. Tragically, the playwright had walked into a trap and the stage was now set for a legal crucifixion, Queensberry persuading Oscar's 'panthers'—either by bribe or bullying—to testify. In court, the 'Red Rose-Leaf' letter was pulled apart and the morals of *Dorian Gray* raked over. On April 5, Queensberry was acquitted and Oscar Wilde was arrested, subsequently charged with gross indecency and sentenced to two years hard labour. It was a Pyrrhic victory for the Screaming Scarlet Marquess, who gnawed at his hat throughout the court proceedings. Not only did Queensberry ruin the sublimely gifted Wilde, he also destroyed the house of Douglas and ensured that Lord Alfred would forever be regarded as Oscar's homme fatale. In her *Ancient Legends,* Speranza expounds upon 'the Clearing,' a ritualised trial of honour, explaining: 'If the accuser has accused . . . out of malice, then may all the evil rest on his head through this life for ever, and may his soul perish everlastingly.' Until his death, the Screaming Marquess would suffer delusions that the 'Oscar-Wilders' were after him. Following a stint in Holloway, Wilde was transferred to Reading Gaol. The conditions were appalling, but he was moved when a fellow prisoner whispered, 'I'm sorry for you, it is harder for the likes of you than it is for the likes of us.' With tears in his eyes, Oscar replied, 'No, my friend, we all suffer alike.'

On February 3, 1896, Wilde had a disturbing dream in which his mother visited his cell but refused to take off her hat or coat. If anyone was going to visit her son in spirit, it was Lady Wilde, whose health had declined with Oscar's incarceration. On her way to the shadow-realm, she had passed as a figment or Fetch in the night. Such visitations are considered ominous portents but surely the worst had already happened? Wilde was in gaol and his mother was dead. Both Speranza and Constance Wilde had more than their fair share of suffering, courtesy of Oscar. In the wake of the scandal, Constance had relocated to Genoa with Cyril and Vyvyan fearing for their safety as public opinion turned against their father. In spite of serious health problems, including incipient spinal paralysis, she travelled from Genoa to England so that her husband would be spared the pain of learning from a stranger of Speranza's death. Recent events had sapped Constance of all vitality, whilst her debilitating condition rendered her 'paralysed without visible weapon,' an eerie reminder of the consequences of breaking the vows of the Golden Dawn.

Mired in despair, Oscar Wilde began his own version of a ritual 'clearing' in the form of a prison letter to Lord Alfred Douglas, the text of which was to become known as *De Profundis* – 'from the depths.' The object of the letter was to teach Bosie 'the meaning of sorrow and its beauty.' And in this Oscar succeeded. However, he was also to write most famously, in *The Ballad of Reading Gaol*, 'Each man kills the thing he loves.' *De Profundis* reveals Wilde still gripped by an abiding passion – beautiful, destructive Bosie, the most capricious and self-centred of all muses, equal in infamy only to Dorian Gray. The playwright had always kept a copy of his mother's *Ancient Legends of Ireland*, which includes a potent segment entitled 'The Power of The Word,' which states, 'No man could escape from the judgement pronounced by a poet over one he desired to injure; for the poet had the knowledge of all the mysteries and was Lord over the secrets of life by the power of The Word.' As he worked on *De Profundis*, the flame of Wilde's imagination illuminated his cell. Although it would not be published in Wilde's lifetime, the missive would ensure that Lord Alfred Douglas would be damned for all eternity. The poet had made his decree; whether he truly intended it to be made public was left to his literary executor, Robbie Ross, who felt no compunction to hold back.

It might have appeared at first that Bosie had got off lightly, decamping to Europe on Wilde's urging. There'd been a warning from the spirits, courtesy of his grandmother Fanny, who had emanated through a 'violently agitated' medium at a séance attended by Lady Queensberry. Sybil managed to get word to her son that he was 'surrounded by powerful enemies' but Lord Alfred would have been heartened to learn that, according to the medium, he had 'good friends in the spirit world.' This was just as well, as Bosie now had few friends in the real world, being widely regarded as the catalyst for Oscar's downfall.

❧

On his release from prison in May 1897, Oscar adopted the pseudonym Sebastian Melmoth, alluding to both saint and sinner. Like Melmoth the playwright was condemned to wander, but his spirit was far from broken and his wit ever sharp. To the consternation of Ross, Constance, and Lady Queensberry, he reunited with Lord Alfred as the summer peaked. In a note to a friend, Oscar exclaimed, 'Bosie is my romance . . . without him my life is dreary.' Lord Alfred cast a potent glamour that Wilde could not resist, kindred to the 'strange and dangerous charm' of Dorian Gray. But the union of the mystical bard and the accursed aristocrat could not sustain with the fates set against them, not to mention the Hotel Royal in Naples, from which they absconded without paying. Next they leased the pretty Villa Giudice, also in Naples, overlooking the sea. Unfortunately, it was overrun by rats and an aged witch, 'muttering incantations . . . and burning odours,' according to Bosie, was called to do a 'house-clearing.' She also read the men's fortunes, Lord Alfred reporting to his mother that, 'Oscar regarded her as a wonderful and powerful sorceress.' The witch's predictions have never been revealed.

On April 7 of the following year Oscar, domiciled in Paris, dreamed of Constance and knew she was dead. The 'grey slowly-moving thing we call Time,' as Wilde would later describe the passing of hours in a letter to Robbie, was running out. Oscar's yearning for Bosie, and vice versa, had finally diminished in Naples, yet they were to remain close until the playwright's demise on November 30, 1900, aged 46. This time it was Oscar who appeared in his own vision. Slipping in and out of consciousness, he told a friend, 'I had an appalling dream. I dreamed I was banqueting with the dead.' 'My dear Oscar,' replied his friend Reggie Turner, 'I'm sure you were the life and soul of the party.'

The fate of Lord Alfred Douglas, who clung on well into the next century, was the destruction of everything he held dear, including those red rose-leaf lips, twisted beyond recognition by the meaning of sorrow.

No matter what he did—from converting to Catholicism, marriage, fatherhood, and the editorship of two newspapers—Lord Alfred was unable to shrug off the past; nor could he forget Oscar, turning out a shelf-load of books on their association. Bosie had been one of the most promising poets of his generation, Wilde describing his sonnets as 'exquisite,' but his prose did not trip gracefully from the page. Tragically for everyone, including himself, Lord Alfred was an accursed Douglas to the core with an unrivalled gift for making enemies. Two of the most verbal were, ironically, former members of the Golden Dawn. Aleister Crowley was the most industrious of them, producing the anti-Bosie leaflet, *The Writing on the Ground*, and the vicious essay 'The Writing on The Wall,' in which he states, 'Bosie is a common prostitute,' and far, far worse. The Beast hoped to drag Bosie into court, but for once Lord Alfred, who was to become litigious in later life, resisted. Crowley also penned a trinity of verses with which to crown Lord Alfred, the rollicking 'A Slim Gilt Soul,' an acrostic ode entitled 'The Child,' and a final offering, 'The Spring of Dirce,' which Crowley dedicated to 'the Divine Oscar.' Bosie also makes a guest appearance as the Earl of Bumble in Crowley's novel *Diary of A Drug Fiend*, and features as the unstable Reggie in Aleister's short story 'An Ideal Idol,' proving that Lord Alfred Douglas was still able to inspire long after his flower-like beauty had faded.

Few are those who have the privilege of reading their own

obituary whilst still alive, and yet this is precisely what happened after Arthur Machen eulogised Bosie in *The Evening News* on February 4, 1921. Under the headline 'A Great Life Spoilt: How the Evil Genius of the Douglases Dogged Lord Alfred,' Bosie was stunned to discover that he had died suddenly from heart failure following a chill. Although Machen is best known for his supernatural work, including *The Great God Pan*, like many a writer he also made a crust from journalism and had been employed by Douglas at his magazine, *The Academy*. There had been an unfortunate dispute over money, leading to Machen lamenting Bosie in print. The epitaph is slender but deadly:

> 'Lord Alfred . . . might have done anything, and, his poetry excepted, he did nothing, and worse than nothing. That charity which is fitting at all times, but most fitting when we are speaking of the newly dead, urges that much should be forgiven this poor, bewildered man, who, with all his gifts, will perhaps only be remembered by the scandals and the quarrels in which he involved himself. It is a great thing, in a sense, to be born a Douglas; but the family inheritance had gifts from evil fairies as well as from good ones.'

Lord Alfred Douglas lived a further twenty-four years after the Machen obituary was published, but socially excommunicated he may as well have already been dead. His name is now barely discernible on his grave although some kind soul has planted a rose-bush close by. As if by design, a shower of rose petals covers the horizontal time mottled stone slab. Unlike Oscar Wilde's extravagant tomb at Père-Lachaise, the silence of the humble cemetery which is Bosie's final resting place belies anything of historical note.

HOW SHALL DEAD MEN SING?
– THE SUPERNATURAL AFFAIR OF
LORD ALFRED DOUGLAS & OSCAR WILDE

'Let me become the scorn of all the wise.
(Out of the East I see the morning ride.)
Thrust if you will, sharp arrows in my side,
Play with my tears and feed upon my sighs.'

– *Lord Alfred Douglas, excerpt from 'Plainte
Eternelle' 1896*

'Then turning to my love, I said
The dead are dancing with the dead,
The dust is whirling with the dust.'

– *Oscar Wilde, excerpt from 'The Harlot's House,'
first published 1885*

Listen. Can you hear them? Rustling like the pages of lost letters,
they are as restless as storm leaves. Pale and paper-thin are the
souls of the uneasy dead. In time's tempest, the forgiven and the
acclaimed are most at peace. The departed artist, who so keenly
made his mark on life remains in death's gothic grey ante-cham-
ber as an inspiration. If celebrated in wordy benedictions by a
succession of biographers, playwrights and film makers, peace-
ful slumbers are assured. The praise-laden creative rests easy in
the tomb and is an influence rather than a haunting. Such is the
posthumous profile of Oscar Wilde, a genius, wit and martyr on
whom no one but the most callous would have wished a prison sentence or an early death. These days, Wilde rightly walks
amongst us as a venerated figure whilst his work continues to

thrive. No need of a haunting for he has transcended earthly woes to become one of culture's towering deities.

But what of the cursed and maligned, those tattered ghosts of ill-repute? Perturbed as orphans, they are the most likely to cast a baleful shadow on the living and whisper their name. Enmeshed between this world and the next, they seek redress. And you will know when they are near. Lights flicker softer than a candle flame, words tumble from the air and books fall open where they are meant to be read in a silent implore. The subtle invasion has commenced. Autumn's final curtsey is their territory, the season of wraiths when death is in the air.

Oscar Wilde's 'Homme Fatale' Lord Alfred Douglas was an autumn baby, born on October 22nd, 1870, to an exceedingly brutish father and a cultured mother possessed of angelic beauty. Little Lord Alfred was raised in the family home, 'Kinmount,' a gloomy neo-Georgian pile set in 30,000 acres of land, with a full complement of servants. It was his charming mother, Sybil, who gave him the nickname 'Boysie' which the child Douglas pronounced 'Bosie.' This pretty soubriquet was to follow him from the nursery to a restless grave. Though cherished by his mother, he was abhorred by his father, the eighth Marquis of Queensberry, John Sholto Douglas, who hailed from a scarlet lineage of notoriously brutal chieftans steeped in corpses, curses and insanity.

They were, as Oscar Wilde would call them, 'A mad, bad, line' whose notable deeds dated as far back as 1298, when William the 'Black Douglas' attempted to fulfil Robert The Bruce's final wish, taking his friend's heart in a silver casket to the Holy Sepulchre in Jerusalem. After setting off, Douglas was fatally ambushed and his remains along with the heart of Robert the Bruce are buried in Melrose Abbey. The emblazoned heart is represented on the Douglas coat of arms. Not all were as valiant as 'The Black Douglas', however. In 1707, the third Marquis of Queensberry murdered a young cook and then roasted him on a spit in the kitchen of Holyrood Palace.

Rumours of a family curse took hold after a series of inexplicably violent deaths. Bosie never got to meet his grandfather, the 7th Marquis, who died on August 6th, 1858, whilst out hunting, when his gun 'accidentally' discharged. *The Evening Herald* reported that 'In sporting circles a belief is expressed that

Honeymoon in Scarlet

the death was not accidental; he had recently sustained severe losses.' One of the most tragic fatalities was that of Bosie's uncle, eighteen year old Francis, who died during a mountaineering expedition in the Swiss Alps. The ropes had not been properly secured during the descent and Francis along with three others plunged 4000 feet of sheer rock face. In desperation, John Sholto Douglas went out ahead of the search party to look for his younger brother but Francis was lost to the desolate gullies of the Matterhorn. It was here that Queensberry forsook God, railing at nature's imperious sovereignty. In the aftermath of the accident, Queen Victoria considered a ban on mountaineering but there are countless other ways in which young men can fall.

Although Queensberry and his wife produced five children, Bosie was the brightest star in his mother's firmament, which served to have heightened his ferocious father's ire. 'Q' as he was often referred to, later wrote of the infant Alfred, 'I cried over you the bitterest tears a man ever shed, that I had brought such a creature into the world.' In *De Profundis*, Wilde's scourging prison letter to Bosie, the captive playwright recounts how the Douglas family considered Queensberry to be an 'Incubus' and had discussed 'getting him put into a lunatic asylum.'

The 'Doom' that Oscar felt was inherent to the Douglas family blood line, where 'Ruin followed like the echo of a bitter cry' was kept at bay from the nursery. Described in Rupert Croft-Cooke's 1963 biography, *Bosie*, as 'an excessively spoilt and notably pretty little boy', Lord Alfred Douglas was a dreamy child who had been taught to love truth and beauty by the doting Lady Queensberry. Unfortunately the disparity between his parents was so vast, it appears to have destabilised their third son who was placed in the position of being Sybil's favourite and Queensberry's most damned. Consequently Bosie was to face a thorny future of absolutes, not absolution. How did that 'slim gilt soul' as Oscar Wilde once described Lord Alfred Douglas in a passionate love letter, become so tarnished not only in his life-time but ever more so in the great here-after? Biographer Caspar Wintermans, who penned the elegant *Alfred Douglas – A Poet's Life & His Finest Work*, described his subject matter as 'A child who should never have been given matches.'

In 1911, Douglas attempted to save his 'slim gilt soul' by converting to Catholicism. Having been mistreated by Queensberry as a child, he was always in need of a mystical father figure. Before Christianity intervened, Bosie's divinity had been Oscar Wilde. The 'Slim Gilt Soul' love-letter written by the playwright in January 1883 continues 'I know Hyacinthus whom Apollo loved so madly was you in Greek days.' The poetic response of Hyacinthus was to follow three years later, when Wilde was behind bars, in a poem called 'Rejected': 'Alas, I have lost my God, My beautiful God Apollo. Wherever his footsteps trod, My feet were wont to follow.' The journey from Apollo to Jesus was to be a torturous one. Of all religions, Catholicism with its dramatic flair, exquisite vestments, elegant rituals and plumes of incense provided decadent repose for heart-weary aesthetes. It was the theatre of the heavens with a crucifixion at its bleeding heart.

Most famously, Aubrey Beardsley capitulated to Catholicism at the end of his life, whilst a death-bed intercession befell Wilde. 'It is when he deals with a sinner that Christ is most romantic' Oscar opined in *De Profundis*. Douglas with many more years of despair ahead must surely have racked up the most prayers: 'And every road leads down from Heaven to Hell/The pearls are numbered on youth's rosary/I have outlived the days desirable/What is there left? And how shall dead men sing...' (*Ennui*)

Sometimes death calls early and is turned away at the door. Praise God thinks the half-drowned man saved from the sea moments before his final breath, but what if this rebuke to mortality alters the course of history, does the rescued one unwittingly continue under a shadow? In his nineteenth year, Lord Alfred Douglas went to Magdalen College, Oxford where he frittered away his days in pleasant trivialities and was amusing company. Charming if study-shy, he had some cards printed that stated – 'Lord Alfred Douglas presents his compliments to .... and regrets that he will be unable to .... in consequences of ....'

Completed, one of these amiable notes would read 'Lord Alfred Bruce Douglas presents his compliments to Professor Smith and regrets that he will be unable to show up an essay on the Evolution of the Moral Idea in consequence of not having prepared one.' But if reduced of content, the card carries its own stark message, namely 'Compliments, regrets and consequences.'

No date has been established when Bosie got trapped under

the ice during his time at Magdalen and nearly drowned. Having led a group of university friends across a frozen river to safety, he then inexplicably jumped on to a block of ice which gave way and plunged him into the freezing water. Watching from the bank, his pals believed he was larking around. In fact Douglas had become trapped under the ice, the delicate hands that Wilde would term as 'nervous' no doubt frantically trying to find a way out. Only one of his friends, 'Tyler' Reid, realised Bosie was in trouble and went to his aid.

Several years later, in a piece called 'Lesser Lights,' which was published in *The English Review*, Lord Alfred mused upon the fate of young noblemen who inherit a title but none of the trappings to sustain them. By this point, Queensberry had sold 'Kinmount' to pay off gambling debts and continue sporting with his many mistresses, much to his long-suffering wife's chagrin. Lady Queensberry divorced her wretched husband on the grounds of cruelty and adultery but the details of his abuse were suppressed in court. This then was the background to the 'Lesser Lights' feature, which eerily parallels Bosie's own watery encounter. Writing of the titled cast-off's 'Ophelia' like destiny, he pondered: 'In how many cases would it not have been better for you if a gentle millstone had been tied around your aristocratic neck, and you had been but firmly lowered into the depths of some glassy stream or frowning tarn, or ornamental sheet of water....'

However, despite the family turmoil, as Rupert Croft-Cooke reports, Bosie was considered during the Magdalen years to be: 'An eager, sporting, rather fast young man, generally liked for his gay and dashing personality.' There was one occasion when having forgotten to bring his football shoes to a game organised by old Winchester school mates; he wore patent leather boots instead. But as Oscar Wilde once quipped, football 'is all very well for rough girls but it is hardly suitable for delicate boys.'

Written in 1890, Bosie's first published attempt at poetry 'Autumn Days' was a slight piece of longing for seasons gone that appeared in *The Oxford Magazine*. Patent leather boots aside, the aesthete in him was awakening, encouraged by his devoted friend, the poet, Lionel Johnson, who was four years his senior. A delicate if resolute young man with an unfortunate predisposition for alcohol, Johnson had dedicated his most passionate sonnet 'A Dream of Youth' to Douglas and was already familiar with London's homosexual underworld but attempted to protect Bosie from it, at least according to biographer, Rupert Croft-Cooke. This is not to say that Lord Alfred Douglas was inexperienced for he was very much a product of the English public school tradition of that era, as Thomas Wright explains in *Oscar's Books*: 'In the late Victorian period homosexual activity was commonplace in all male educational establishments such as Oxford University and public schools.'

Although it has been suggested that Lionel and Alfred may have been lovers, the poet didn't disclose his extracurricular activities as Croft-Cooke explained in his 1963 biography, 'Johnson, who sincerely loved and respected Bosie, did not discuss the squalid world he was discovering.' Nonetheless, a letter written by Lord Alfred during Wilde's incarceration contradicts this: 'So far from his (OW) leading me astray it was I that (unwittingly) pushed him over the precipice.' However, it could be argued that Alfred and Oscar held hands in a mutually destructive tryst. Though married, Wilde had commenced a relationship with Robbie Ross around 1886. Under no circumstances could Ross compete with the élan of Lord Alfred Douglas and the pair were to be set on a lengthy collision course. Having been dunked in the fountain at King's College Oxford by fellow students for disrespecting the university, Ross had headed for London where he began to infiltrate literary life. Lionel Johnson described him thus: 'What be his morals, I know not, himself is delightful.'

There is in the Wilde/Douglas union an uncanny sense of predestination, as if their roles had already been written long before they met. Words were to bring them together and be their undoing. In the same year that Bosie's melancholy 'Autumn Days' was published, Oscar met Lionel Johnson at Oxford, upon the recommendation of Walter Pater. It was Johnson who gave Douglas his first copy of *The Picture of Dorian Gray*. The next would be signed by its author, Oscar Wilde. A supernatural masterpiece, *The Picture of Dorian Gray* tells the story of an innocent aristocrat who has his portrait painted by the artist, Basil Hallward, at the height of his beauty. Dorian is then seduced by the decadent doctrines of the sophisticated Lord Henry Wotton, which leads to his moral ruin, the evidence of the young man's sins manifesting on the increasingly terrifying portrait but not on his eternally youthful form.

> 'Dorian Gray stepped up on the dais, with the air of a young Greek martyr and made a little moue of discontent to Lord Henry, to whom he had rather taken a fancy. He was so unlike Basil. They made a delightful contrast. And he had such a beautiful voice. After a few moments, he said to him, "have you really a very bad influence, Lord Henry? As bad as Basil says?" "There is no such thing as a good influence, Mr Gray. All influence is immoral."'

The book features a trinity of central characters with specific roles, namely Dorian Gray as temptation, the voice of conscience as Basil Hallward and Henry Wotton as the catalyst for disaster.

Is fate written before we even turn the page? It is not surprising that many readers of this imaginative novel have supposed that Dorian Gray was based on the character of Lord Alfred Douglas. It is uncanny that it was written before the two men met. Although Dorian's surname is attributable to the handsome poet, John Gray, who Wilde had befriended, the name Douglas derives from the Celtic for 'dark grey.' The description of Dorian Gray, with his gilt hair and delicately clear features, is identical to the appearance of the young nobleman during his Oxford years. Bosie's mother was called Sybil, the same name as the actress who loved Dorian with a fatal passion. The Sibyls of ancient Greek and Roman legend were oracles that made their predictions from different holy sites.

How easily the portents aligned. *The Picture of Dorian Gray* cast a dark glamour on all the protagonists in the unfolding drama and helped to set the stage for a tragedy of Shakespearian proportions. Prior to having met the book's author, Bosie confessed to having read *Dorian Gray* fourteen times. He would also describe it as being used as an agent of 'black magic' by Wilde, for purposes of seduction. Oscar Wilde knew all too well the power of language having once stated: 'Words! mere words! How terrible they were! What a subtle magic there was in them! They seemed to be able to give a plastic form to formless things.' Indeed it was magical words, a spell cast by Wilde in *Dorian Gray* that was to bring the twenty year old Lord Alfred Douglas to his door in the company of Lionel Johnson on a summer's afternoon in June 1891.

How potent was Wilde's wordy ritual. Does it need to be said that Lord Alfred Douglas was Oscar's ideal? Dorian personified? The catastrophe would never have taken place had he not been. 'You are the divine thing I want, the thing of grace and genius,' the smitten sorcerer would write to Bosie during their courtship. As Philippe Julian states in *Dreamers of Decadence*: 'Around Wilde there was formed an ideal of male beauty which was close to the idea created in Rossetti's studio twenty years before. Lord Alfred Douglas is the counterpart of Elizabeth Siddal.... (Rossetti's wife and muse) Perhaps Wilde fell in love with Lord Alfred because he resembled, in rather more robust form, Burne-Jones' models and above all Watt's knights.'

Poor Lionel Johnson would come to bitterly regret being the conduit for the fatal meeting of Bosie and Oscar but destiny hurried them along to the Wilde home at 16 Tite Street, Chelsea. Oscar would have most certainly received them in his library. Aged 36 and with his literary star rising, Wilde was a fashionable figure with an imposing air. Though *Dorian Gray* had caused consternation in some quarters, Oscar Wilde was rapidly striving towards an ambition that he had once shared with a university friend, Hunter Blair, 'I'll be a poet, a writer, a dramatist. Somehow or other, I'll be famous, and if not famous, notorious.' One wonders which hand he proffered to Bosie in greeting but the difference was distinct. During a palm reading by Count Louis Harmon, he had been told 'The left hand is the hand of a king but the right that of a king who will send himself into exile.'

Upstairs, Wilde's wife of six years, Constance, tended to their two young sons, Cyril and Vyvyan. She was a sombre beauty with a bright mind. Much disparagment has been cast on Oscar's affection for Constance. However as Wilde's delightful poem 'To My Wife' attests, this was no mere marriage of convenience but one with a great depth of tenderness. Nevertheless, with his questing spirit and voracious mind Wilde was a cultural gourmand and he had grown bored of domesticity. As was customary with guests, Wilde would have taken Alfred and Lionel upstairs to meet his wife. Constance no doubt would have been relieved for as she was said to have remarked 'Since Oscar wrote

Dorian Gray, no one will speak to us.'

Constance, who Wilde described as a 'violet-eyed Artemis' was not the docile naive creature she is often portrayed as, but was a learned, curious young woman. On November 13th, 1888, she had been initiated into the magical order of The Golden Dawn. Fellow members included W.B Yeats, Aleister Crowley and Arthur Machen. In taking her vows, she would have sworn never to reveal The Golden Dawn's secrets under 'pain of being paralysed without visible weapon.' At the time of the inception of *Dorian Gray* Constance would have been a member of the Golden Dawn, biographer John Murray suggesting in *The Tragic and Scandalous Life of Mrs Oscar Wilde* that she discussed the order's rituals with her husband, thus breaking her vows.

In *De Profundis* Wilde wrote of: 'The note of doom that like a purple thread runs through the texture of *Dorian Gray*.' This was not discernible on that gentle June day, yet the fates were already busy at the loom. By the time Robbie Ross received a letter written by Oscar Wilde from the Royal Palace Hotel, Kensington, in which he waxed lyrically, 'Bosie is quite like a narcissus – so white and gold. He lies like a hyacinth on the sofa and I worship him,' the design of the fatal friendship had taken full form.

Wilde had largely absented himself from the family home and was taking rooms in hotels or chambers, wherein Bosie was inevitably to be gracefully draped. Never was destiny so hard at work upon such a star-crossed tapestry. The lovers passed through a tumultuous period: 'those two and a half years during which the fates were weaving into one scarlet pattern the threads of our divided lives,' Wilde noted in *De Profundis*.

Love like fate is often blind and so were the main protagonists. Lord Alfred Douglas, in those early days, often took the slighted Robbie Ross out and about with him, believing him to be a friend. It is a mark of Ross's tact that he was able to suppress his true feelings. Douglas was without guile, a gregarious, impetuous young man who had caught the heart of one of the most fashionable figures in London, whilst Ross had been relegated to an occasionally referenced foot-note in Oscar's life.

From the opening night of 'Lady Windermere's Fan' at the St James Theatre in February 1892, which was to prove a runaway success, the playwright's every move was a continual source of fascination to the press. Wilde was beginning his ascendency and Lord Alfred Douglas was his very visible companion. Intoxicated by each other's company, they rode the whirlwind, deaf to the rising murmurs of gossip and in certain quarters, envy. Oscar Wilde had wooed the younger man with a six month campaign as Bosie later admitted to the writer, H.Montgomery Hyde; 'He (OW) continually asked me to lunch and to dine with him...sending letters, notes and telegrams. He flattered me, gave me presents and made much of me in every way. He gave me copies of all his books with inscriptions in them.' Bosie in turn was bewitched by Oscar's art and his unsurpassable gift for conversation in which the listener was entranced by Wilde's mellifluous voice. 'I have never known anyone to come near him,' Douglas confided to Montgomery Hyde. 'He did succeed in weaving spells. One sat and listened to him enthralled. It all appeared to be Wisdom and Power and Beauty and Enchantment. It was indeed enchantment and nothing else.'

Though there was a thriving creative homosexual milieu in London, Victorian England was steeped in hypocrisy and homophobia. Wilde and Douglas were sexual outlaws, a couple when homosexuality was illegal. Oscar Wilde's predilection for male prostitutes and rough trade, which he termed 'feasting with panthers' made them easy marks for blackmail but the playwright was drunk on fame and Bosie had the recklessness of an aristocrat. Much like the spectral Dorian Gray, they reaped the pleasures of the underworld, little understanding how vicious it could be. One should also spare a thought for the young men with whom they dallied, who were often of poor means and dazzled by the privilege they glimpsed. No excuse for blackmail although as one of the 'panthers,' Robert Cliburn, explained to Wilde: 'There is good and bad in every one of us.'

Though Dorian Gray overshadows the Douglas/Wilde tryst, another of Wilde's fictional characters, Lord Arthur Saville, also exerted an influence albeit to a far minor degree. Early on in the relationship, Oscar had presented a copy of 'Lord Arthur Saville's Crime' to Bosie. The story of a youthful aristocrat who has his palm read to disastrous affect, the cautionary tale reiterated Oscar's superstitious nature.

It is significant that Wilde was born into a family who took seriously the 'unseen.' His father, Sir William Robert Wills

Wilde, a renowned surgeon, had penned a volume of folklore entitled *Irish Popular Superstitions*, whilst his mother, Lady Jane Francesca Wilde, otherwise known as 'Speranza,' collated *Legends, Charms & Superstitions of Ireland*. Wilde understood the nature of enchantment and declined membership of the '13' club, who sought to debunk superstition by arranging dinners with a '13' theme which included thirteen guests at 13 tables raising 13 toasts. He wrote to the '13' club's leading light, Mr W.H. Blanch, explaining his reason for turning down the invitation; 'They (superstitions) are the colour elements of thought and imagination. They are the opposite of common sense. Common sense is the enemy of romance. The aim of your society seems to be dreadful. Leave us some unreality.' Though not as florid as Oscar in his otherworldly beliefs, Bosie was wary of ill-omens refusing to go out on Friday 13th, whilst his mother, like many Victorians, attended séances. Given the sorry consequences brought about by Lord Arthur's palm reading, a little reticence might have been prudent, but Oscar regularly consulted psychics. Yet again, Wilde's future was given dubious clarity as Vincent O'Sullivan reports in *Aspects of Wilde*: 'He (OW) told me that three or four years before his imprisonment he had his palm read by a fortune-teller. The fortune teller told him quite correctly some events of his past, and then added: 'I see a very brilliant life for you up to a certain point. Then I see a wall. Beyond the wall I see nothing.'

The quickening pace of the Wilde-Bosie story reads like a gallivant to the gallows. Their story possessed the gothic ambience of Oscar's macabre poem 'The Harlot's House': 'We watched the ghostly dancers spin, To sound of horn and violin, Like black leaves wheeling in the wind. Like wire-pulled automatons, Slim silhouetted skeletons, Went sliding through the slow quadrille, They took each other by the hand...'

Inevitably their own circle began to take sides in the dance. Like Robbie Ross, the poet Lionel Johnson wasn't happy with the union of Oscar and Douglas but he didn't hide his dismay. In his 1967 book, *Feasting with Panthers*, Rupert Croft-Cooke observed 'When Bosie came under the fashionable spell of Wilde, Johnson found him unbearable and wrote a sonnet to Wilde who had once been his idol.' The elegy, entitled 'The Destroyer of a Soul' is as harrowing as the banshee's wail: '... Mourning for that live soul, I used to see; Soul of a saint, whose friend I used to be: Till you came by! A cold, corrupting fate'... The poem ends on the equally damning 'Go, ring the death bell with a deep, triumphant toll! Say you, my friend sits by me still? Ah peace! Call you this thing my friend? This nameless thing? This living body, hiding its dead soul?' The searing tone is at odds with Johnson's usually considered style and there may well have been an element of jealousy directed at Wilde who was now Bosie's closest companion. Lionel's own future was to be a tragic one and he never resolved his differences with Oscar. He did however stay in contact with Bosie and went so far as to arrange a tutor for him, Campbell Dodgson.

Though well-read, Lord Alfred Douglas had never been the scholarly type and distractions there were all too many. Any serious study with Dodgson was derailed when in February 1893 they went to stay with Wilde at Babbacombe Cliff in Torquay. Dodgson would picturesquely describe the scene in a letter; 'Our life is lazy and luxuriant; our moral principles lax. We argue for hours in favour of different interpretations of Platonism. Oscar implores me with outspread arms and tears in his eyes to let my soul alone and cultivate my body for six weeks. Bosie is beautiful and fascinating but quite wicked.'

Much has been made by 'Bosie-Bashers' (a term coined by his biographer, Caspar Wintermans) of the fact that Lord Alfred Douglas subsequently dropped out of university without getting a degree, that he lived only for the moment, transported by art and pleasure. In preparation for his study time, Dodgson noted of his charge; 'Bosie was in a whirl; he had no books, no money, no cigarettes and had omitted to send many telegrams of the first importance.' After several whirling weeks Dodgson left Torquay and the storm clouds gathered.

For all the revelries, there were combustible elements to the Douglas-Wilde alliance and whilst at Babbacombe, they had their first fight, which was recorded in *De Profundis* as 'Revolting.' Most couples quarrel but it is not within such an incendiary context as love outside the law, and this was further compounded by the temperaments involved. Bosie's hot-headed petulance vied with Wilde's dramatic self-aggrandisement. Of that first argument, Rupert Croft-Cooke adds a note of insightful conjecture: 'It may have started with something quite trivial. Bosie had a habit, distressing to Oscar, of not taking him quite as seriously as he would have liked either as a King of Life or a Lord of Language, in fact mischievously pulling his leg at times. For instance, Bosie had given him for his last birthday a turquoise set in diamonds which he wore in his shirt front. Bosie considered it rather ostentatious and since there was talk at the time of that famous blue stone, the Hope diamond, he called it the 'Hope-Not,' a crack which infuriated Oscar not by its feebleness but for its implications. Though Wilde may have felt piqued by Bosie's daft quip, for that's all it was, the Hope diamond was believed to have been an accursed gem that brought ruin to all associated with it.

If Bosie was to leave any impression of worth at Oxford it was in his editorship of a student paper, *The Spirit Lamp*, which he tended with flair and good humour. As well as including contributions from Wilde, Lionel Johnson, Robbie Ross and the morbid snake bedecked Count Stenbock, volume 3 of *The Spirit Lamp* also contained a rather gloomy poem by none other than Queensberry that concluded: 'Yes, all must die: repine not, Death but returns us where, We came from in the silence: – And perfect rest is there.'

Bosie had introduced Wilde to his father in November, 1892, at the Café Royal. Alfred and Oscar had been dining when 'Q' entered the establishment. Rather bravely, Bosie approached his father and invited him over. Wilde with his customary charm had proved so entertaining the normally belligerent Marquis had a very pleasant time. Bosie's mother was less easily appeased and had written a letter expressing her concern about her son's association with Wilde to the President of Magdalen College.

In the lull before he quit Magdalen, Lord Alfred penned a review of Wilde's play, 'Salomé', for *The Spirit Lamp*. In thrall to Huysman's decadent gem *A rebours*, which had influenced *Dorian Gray*, Wilde had written *Salomé* in French. Attempts to produce the play with Sarah Bernhardt in the title role had been scuppered by censorious attitudes to the biblical content. Concluding the review, Bosie remarked: 'Anyone, therefore, who suffers from that most appalling and widespread of diseases which takes the form of a morbid desire for health had better flee from Salomé or they will surely get a shock.....' It was a decidedly decadent farewell to Oxford. For once, his parents were united in opinion, shocked by their son's educational swan-dive. Needless to say, Oscar was more magnanimous, comparing Bosie to Shelley and Swinburne, who had not gained degrees but had soared as poets. 'Tell me not of Philosophies, Of morals, ethics, laws of life; Give me no subtle theories, No instruments of wordy strife' Douglas had written in a poem entitled 'Apologia' in his last year at Magdalen.

One usually seeks to keep loved ones out of trouble, but Oscar set Bosie a new project: to translate *Salomé* into English. The book was to be published by John Lane with illustrations by Aubrey Beardsley whom Wilde had daubed 'The Silver Hatchet' on account of his striking profile. Though very different from *Dorian Gray*, certain themes hold true to both works including a trinity of central characters with similar purpose, namely Salomé the temptress, the voice of the conscience, John The Baptist a.k.a Jokanaan and the catalyst for disaster, Herod the tetrarch. The play is saturated in scarlet and evil presage, as Herod announces:

'Remember, I slipped in blood when I entered. Also I heard a beating of wings in the air, a beating of mighty wings. These are very evil omens, and there are others, I am sure there were others.'

And indeed there were. Lord Alfred would have commenced work on *Salomé* in the aftermath of yet another shocking family tragedy. Bosie's uncle James, an alcoholic with an unusual attachment to his sister, Florrie, had slit his own throat with a razor in front of a mirror at the Euston Station Hotel. In the play's opening sequence, the Captain of the Guard attempts to dissuade Salomé from her fatal pursuit of Jokanaan, but he fails and kills himself. Shocked by his sudden demise, the page to Herodius cries out 'He was my brother, and nearer to me than a brother.' The scenario foresees the death of Bosie's beloved older brother, Francis, Viscount Drumlanrig, the following year. The title 'Drumlanrig' originally bestowed upon the family by James 1st and given to the first born male of each successive Douglas line was particularly unlucky. The sequence of misfortune commenced after the 3rd duke died along with his wife when his pistol exploded and his successor perished with his horse when they fell into a fast-moving river. The Drumlanrig blight continued to ricochet down the centuries, taking countless into unhappy graves, until it reached Francis, who was fatally wounded when his gun misfired whilst out hunting. A former Lieutenant in the Coldstream Guards, 'Francy' had been appointed as a private assistant to the Foreign Secretary, Lord Rosebery. Believing that his son and Rosebery were romantically involved, Queensberry threatened to horse-whip the Foreign Secretary. He desisted due to the intervention of the Prince of Wales. At the time of Viscount Drumlanrig's death, Rosebery had risen to become Prime Minister. Rumours persisted that Francis was being blackmailed over his alleged affair with Rosebery and had in fact committed suicide.

There were so many heads served up on silver platters and there would be more to come. By the end of August, 1893, Bosie had completed the translation of *Salomé* but Wilde made so many changes to his work, Douglas was unhappy and they quarrelled. Robert Ross meanwhile was waiting patiently on the side-lines for just such an occurrence. Always ready to capitalise on any discord between Wilde and Bosie, he suggested that Aubrey Beardsley should take over as translator but his attempt was less than pleasing. Ultimately, Wilde liked his own work best. The evidence of the complicity between Aubrey and Robbie is borne out in a letter the illustrator sent to Ross '… I suppose you've heard all about the Salomé Row. I can tell you I had a warm time of it between Lane and Oscar and Co. For one week the numbers of telegraph and messenger boys who came to the door was simply scandalous. I really don't quite know how the matter really stands now. Anyhow Bozie's (sic) name is not to turn up on the title… By the way Bozie is going to Egypt in what capacity I don't quite gather; something diplomatic I fancy. Have you heard from either him or Oscar? Both of them are really very dreadful people.' The final line was an unusually even-handed if withering comment from 'The Silver Hatchet' as opinions on the Douglas-Wilde tryst tended to be divided, mostly against Bosie.

During this period, Oscar was working intermittently on *An Ideal Husband* and had taken rooms at 10 St. James Place to concentrate on the play. In *De Profundis* Wilde admonishes

Lord Alfred for interrupting his writing schedule with 'chat and cigarettes' not to mention demanding lunch – with liqueurs – at the Café Royal or the Berkeley. 'We did not separate as a rule until after midnight as supper at Willis's had to wind up the entrancing day. That was my life for those three months, every single day.' If Douglas was nonchalant about his louche life, Wilde was becoming a tad worried and expressed his concerns in a letter to Lady Queensberry in which he observed 'Bosie seems to me be in a very bad state of health. He is sleepless, nervous and rather hysterical. He seems to me to be quite altered... he does absolutely nothing and is quite astray in life, and may, unless you or Drumlanrig do something, come to grief of some kind.'

Wilde suggested that Bosie might benefit from going abroad. Sybil Queensberry reached out to the Consul-General of Egypt, Lord Cromer, who was married to one of her oldest friends, Ethel. A plan was devised that would appeal to Bosie; a break in Cairo with Lord and Lady Cromer, which Sybil hoped might rouse her son's interest in a future as an attaché in the diplomatic service, far from the distractions of London. She made Wilde promise that he would not follow Lord Alfred to Cairo.

'Over a palm tree's top I see the peaks, Of the tall pyramids; and though my eyes are barred from it, I know that on the sand, Crouches a thing of stone that in some wise Broods on my heart; and from the darkening land Creeps Fear and to my soul in whisper speaks.' (Extract from *The Sphinx*, British Agency, Cairo, January 1894) Had Lady Queensberry's plan worked, she might have averted the greatest scandal of the Fin de Siècle. Lives and reputations would have been saved, including that of her son. At twentythree, Bosie was very much a product of privilege, a blithe voluptuary with little understanding of conspiring forces, and yet his poem 'The Sphinx' written during his Egyptian sojourn, suggests that all was not well. 'There are times when my heart aches' he would write to his mother from Cairo 'and my eyes fill with tears at the sense of the pitiableness of my position and the darkness of my future.'

After three months with the Cromers, he palled up with Reggie Turner, aspiring writer Robert Hichens, and published author E.F Benson in Luxor. There were rides out to the pyramids, a trip down the Nile, visits to the bazars and (untrue) rumours sprang up of a brief liaison between Douglas and Lord

Kitchener, whose stern moustachioed face was to adorn World War 1 recruitment posters. If his country didn't need Bosie, he ardently believed that Oscar did and a volley of correspondence continued with his mother, who feared for her son's very soul and wrote to tell him so. Once again, *Dorian Gray* returned to the frame. In a response from Bosie to Lady Queensberry, dated January 6th, 1894, he attempted to allay her distress:

'*Dorian Gray* is a book of exaggerated types. It is all supernatural and unreal. Nobody wants to murder anyone else's soul, the whole idea and your whole attitude is really morbid and hysterical, you have created for yourself this imaginary tragedy that has no real existence at all. I verily believe that if Oscar had not written or you had never read *Dorian Gray*, these ideas would never have occurred to you at all. It appears to me that the enormous power of the sort of uncanny half real half fantastic atmosphere of the book has got hold of your soul and made it a little mad. Oscar has no desire to ruin my soul in order that he may have the pleasure of getting a morbid satisfaction from the contemplation of its ruin. He is merely a very brilliant and very irresponsible and very impulsive creature who is very fond of me.'

However Sybil was not convinced and she moved swiftly. With the help of Lord Cromer a post as an honorary attaché to Lord Currie, the Ambassador in Constantinople was arranged for Douglas. Lord Cromer gave Bosie the news but he failed to understand that he was meant to take the role immediately. Under the mistaken belief that the position would remain open, Bosie wired Wilde and a French rendezvous was arranged. Although Oscar would eviscerate the Paris reunion in *De Profundis*, it went well enough for the two men to return to London and resume their relationship. Unfortunately, news of the assignation filtered back to an infuriated Lord Currie. Any chance of Bosie enjoying a distinguished overseas career was dashed. One can only imagine his mother's anguish, for what is a soul dipped in gilt but an ornament?

For Wilde and Douglas, the pre-dominant shades of 1894 were to be green and scarlet. Decadent literature, of which

Dorian Gray might be considered the jewel in the multi-hued crown, was informed by the desire to create new sensations. In decadent writing, colours served to heighten the mood or act as in the case of Dorian's surname as an indication of character; hence he is neither black or white, good or bad. On his return from Egypt, Robert Hichens penned a satire entitled *The Green Carnation* starring Bosie as the narcissistic Lord Reginald Hastings who resembles a Burne-Jones angel and Wilde as the inexhaustibly witty author, Esme Amarinth. The book's title refers to the penchant of Parisian homosexuals for wearing dyed green carnations, which Wilde and his followers took up. Green however is also the colour of envy. A minor journalist, Hichens conceived of the book whilst in Luxor, hoping that he would achieve the same literary success as fellow guest E.F Benson.

Unaware of Hichen's inky machinations, Lord Alfred had introduced him to Wilde in London. *The Green Carnation* is largely intended as a light-hearted parody, Esme proclaiming at dinner 'Ah here are our devilled kidneys. I suppose you and I are devilled Reggie. People say we are so wicked.' Nevertheless, there is an undertone of trepidation regarding Reggie's imperilled character as perceived by one Madame Valtesi: 'Now, think of Lord Reggie. He is one of the most utterly vicious young men of the day Why? Because like the chameleon, he takes his colour from whatever he rests upon or is put near. And he has been put near scarlet instead of white.' At the close of the book, the kindly Lady Locke who realises that Lord Hastings is only proposing to her for her money tells him 'I can never love an echo. And you are an echo.' The chapter concludes with Reggie giving Esme a (slim) gold tipped cigarette and they depart to the city. Needless to say, *The Green Carnation* did not please Queensberry, whose fictional other is briefly depicted in conflict with his son. Nothing could have been closer to the truth. Ironically, Q again encountered his son in the company of Wilde at the Café Royal but this time he was not to be charmed. He was already wielding a horse-whip for Rosebery and the chance meeting at the Café Royal pushed him over the edge. In his book *The Wilde Album* Oscar's grandson, Merlin Holland, states that one of the playwright's notes to Douglas... 'had fallen into the Marquis's hands in which he had written "it is a marvel that those red-rose leaf lips of yours should be made no less for music of song than

Robert Hichen's witty satire featuring Bosie as the flighty Lord
Reginald Hastings & his friend, the perpetually amusing author,
Esme Araminth. The book was withdrawn before Oscar Wilde's
trial, so as not to be prejudicial.

for madness of kisses.'" Not a man to be concerned with dates, Queensberry scribbled a furious letter to Lord Alfred on April 1st, 1894, in which he threatened to disown him if he didn't end intimacies with Wilde. The livid missive concluded with a warning that the enraged Marquis would be justified in shooting the playwright.

Do we all unwittingly dance to the same song as our ancestors? The beating of the terrible wings of the 'Mad, bad' Queensberry line was finally audible, like the sound of drummer boys before battle. Lord Alfred Douglas was now officially at war with his father. He responded to Queensberry with a seven word telegram that would become infamous: 'What a funny little man you are.' Its condemnatory simplicity belies the fact that Bosie was frightened of his father and he subsequently purchased a gun. How could he have not? To do so was already written in his accursed heritage. Responding to his son's telegram, Queensberry thundered: 'I will give you the thrashing you deserve. Your only excuse is that you must be crazy. I hear from a man at Oxford that you were thought crazy there and that accounts for a good deal that has happened. If I catch you again with that man (Wilde) I will make a public scandal in a way you little dream of...' If fate is preordained, then Douglas and Wilde, the scarlet butterfly and the emerald dandy, were its hostages. In *De Profundis*, Oscar perceived Bosie as the heir of misfortune who had ensnared him on destiny's web:

'I need not go on further into the strange doom you seem to have brought on me in all things big or little. It makes me feel sometimes as if you yourself had been merely a puppet worked by some secret and unseen hand to bring terrible events to a terrible issue. But puppets themselves have passion. They will bring a new plot into what they are presenting and twist the ordered issue of vicissitude to suit some whim or appetite of their own. To be entirely free, and at the same time entirely dominated by law.'

The unshakable decree or 'law' – cast who knew when – was upon Bosie's eldritch blood-line. Potent curses afflicting ancient families cast long shadows. As hostilities escalated between father and son, Lady Queensberry attempted to intercede, packing Lord Alfred off to Florence in the belief that Wilde would remain in London but the playwright was unable to resist his 'âme damnée.' Whilst in Italy, Oscar commenced working on 'A Florentine Tragedy.' Although the play was never completed, 'A Florentine Tragedy' appears to touch on recent events when the noble Guido speaks of the unseemly Simone, describing him as 'A windy brawler in a world of words. I never met so eloquent a fool,' which points to Queensberry's opening salvo on April fool's day. Back in London, Wilde consulted a solicitor about 'The windy brawler' but no further action was taken. A month later, Queensberry, with a prize-fighter in tow, barged into Wilde's Tite Street home, spewing allegations. In retort, Wilde and Douglas made sure they were seen out together as often as possible but the irascible Queensberry hounded them, determined to crush Wilde and his son.

Despite all of the impending portents, these were Oscar's glory days, as Holbrook Jackson noted in *The Eighteen Nineties*:

> 'He was a monarch in his own sphere, rich, famous, popular; looked up to as a master by the younger generation, courted by the fashionable world, loaded with commissions by theatrical managers, interviewed, paragraphed and pictured by the press and envied by the envious and incompetent. All the flattery and luxury of success were his and his luxuriant and applause loving nature appeared to revel in the glittering surf of conquest like a joyous bather in a sunny sea. But it was only a partial victory. The apparent capitulation of the upper and middle classes was illusory, and even the man in the street who heard about him and wondered was moved by an uneasy suspicion that all was not well.'

When Bosie's gun went off accidentally at the Berkeley hotel, it anticipated Viscount Drumlanrig's death on October 8th, by mere months. Truly the Queensberry curse was biting at their heels. Wilde gave Douglas some flowers to place on his brother's grave. As for Lord Alfred, described by Max Beerbohm as 'obviously mad, like all his family'; in those rare quiet moments when he wasn't engaged in vituperative correspondence with his malevolent father or being whisked away to the land of enchantment by Wilde, he found solace in his poetry. The most tender of his sonnets written that year, 'In Memorium,' was dedicated to Francis... 'In this short armistice From my soul's war against the bitter throng Of present woes, let these poor lines be strong In love enough to bear a brother's kiss....'

But the fracture that had existed all his life, amplified by the polarities between his mother and father and now between Queensberry and Wilde, manifested in the extraordinary 'Two Loves', which was to become Douglas' best known poem. Although a homosexual allegory containing the famous line 'The love that dares not speak its name,' the strange garden in which the two figures wander, so very distant from one another, might also be a reflection of Lord Alfred's torn psyche. At best, Bosie could be described as acutely capricious. Addressing the younger man's propensity for mood-change in a letter, Wilde gave a typically poetic diagnosis; '...the delicate fancy of your genius, so surprising always in its sudden swallow-flights towards north and south, towards sun and moon...'

As Queensberry continued his campaign of intimidation, Wilde consulted 'The Sybil of Mortimer Street' otherwise known as Mrs Robinson, who foresaw a nice long voyage. Both Wilde and Bosie believed this to be the vacation they took to Algiers in January, 1895. All divination is open to interpretation, though Mrs Robinson was categorical, in March 1895, that Wilde would 'triumph.' He would indeed 'triumph' as a revered historical figure and as a great artist, but unfortunately for Wilde however, he assumed that Mrs Robinson was predicting imminent victory over Queensberry and not the far-flung future. Both Oscar and Lord Alfred Douglas were born under the sign of Libra and their correlating charts share many of the same aspects. Ruled by Venus, Librans have an acute appreciation of beauty and are often drawn to the theatre, opera and ballet. In Greek mythology, Libra is represented by Astraea, the goddess of justice who weighs the lives of mortal men. Now both Oscar Wilde and Lord Alfred Douglas were to be put in the dock, one in person, the other by implication. The consequences were to be ruinous for both, though the punishments were to be very different.

On February 18th, 1895, Queensberry had left a card for

Wilde at the Albermarle club, accusing him of 'Posing as a somdomite.' (sic) The gesture was one of public libel and Wilde acted, consulting a solicitor. A warrant was issued for the arrest of 'Q.' It is now that the scarlet and purple threads of the story become too thickly interwoven to deftly unpick in a single stroke.

Subsequently, in *De Profundis*, he would label Bosie as the 'evil genius' behind his downfall but the imprisoned Wilde was not in his right mind at the time. One could just as likely blame Dorian Gray, who would also take his turn in court, deemed 'immoral and indecent.' Bosie-Bashers perceive that Lord Alfred urged Wilde to take action against his father, to get back at Queensberry. This unfortunately is born out in *De Profundis* but the proof of Wilde's (understandable) mental instability at the time of writing the letter is apparent in one peculiar phrase where Douglas and Dorian finally become one in Oscar's tortured mind; 'When I wrote in my aphorisms that it was simply the feet of clay that made the gold of the image precious, it was of you that I was thinking.' This derives from *The Picture of Dorian Gray* but Douglas was not yet known to Wilde when he wrote the book so how could he have been thinking of Bosie?

The case for 'Regina versus Queensberry' was set for April 3rd. It would have been a year and a day since Bosie received Queensberry's first fuming epistle. A year and a day has always had magical significance and is the time given in pagan relationships before a couple commit to a 'hand-fasting' ceremony and are bound together. Traditionally, the commonest time span for bewitched mortals to spend in the land of the fey is a year and a day. In feudal England, if a serf managed to be on the run from the lord of the land for a year and a day, he would be a free man. Queensberry, who had always neglected Bosie, may nonetheless have still been possessive of his son and envious of the affection in which he held Oscar Wilde. The disastrous trinity took their places, the voice of the conscience, Oscar, the catalyst for disaster, Queensberry, and in the role of temptation, Lord Alfred Douglas.

Paying for the cost of the court case had been a communal effort, with Wilde, Bosie and his brother Percy as well as business man and ally, Ernest Leverson, all chipping in. At least some of the legal fund was frittered on a short holiday in Monte Carlo by Oscar and Bosie, the young aristocrat taking to the gaming tables with relish. Wilde would later berate Bosie as the instigator of the mini-break in *De Profundis* but he went of his own accord. Were they desperate, crazy, oblivious or naive? Bosie was sure that if he could just tell the jury what a vicious rotter his father was, all would be resolved in their favour. As Caspar Wintermans observed, however, in *A Poet's Life and His Work*, Douglas had...'Not the slightest idea of jurisprudence, he was but 24... and incapable of adequately judging the situation' or many others for that matter. Furthermore, Oscar's advocates had advised against Bosie going into the witness box, a decision Douglas would rail against for the rest of his life.

Wilde returned from Monte Carlo to face the bleak news that Queensberry's legal team had rounded up the 'panthers' to testify against him. Some had been bribed, others intimidated into giving the most damning of statements. In underestimating 'the windy brawler' Wilde had walked into a trap, with more scarlet and purple strands than could have been anticipated, including a counter-plot that Queensberry had agreed to supress certain details of Viscount Drumlanrig's relationship with Rosebery, if the government delivered the playwright's head on a silver platter via the British 'justice' system. Perhaps there were additional reasons why Lord Alfred Douglas had purchased a gun as he and his brother were moving targets in a very dangerous set of circumstances. We will never know what information they had shared. Lord Alfred Douglas would declare after the trial that the guilty verdict was: 'The sacrifice of a great poet to save a degraded band of politicians.'

Why did Wilde pursue his course of action to prosecute Queensberry? Once again, *Dorian Gray* may hold the answer: 'I have always been my master; had at least always been so, till I met Dorian Gray. Then – but I don't know how to explain it to you. Something seemed to tell me that I was on the verge of a terrible crisis in my life. I had a strange feeling that fate had in store for me exquisite joys and exquisite sorrows.' Nevertheless, Wilde – used to success – whose life had so far been a winning performance, believed he could convince a jury. This tragically was not to be case. In court an accursed book and an accursed blood-line converged, the charge led by a slavering Marquis. Pages of 'Dorian' were read out to the jury along with Wilde's love letters to Lord Alfred Douglas, some of the most beautiful words ever written from one man to another, decimated for their content along with the reputation of sender and recipient and then the 'panthers' were unleashed. Only Alfred Taylor valiantly refused to turn queen's evidence and as a consequence was also laid open to charges. The case collapsed: Queensberry emerged victorious, the voice of righteous morality, the tables turned on Wilde who was no longer simply 'posing' as a sodomite.

Lord Alfred Douglas, Robbie Ross and Reggie Turner implored Wilde to leave the country whilst he could. In 1936, author Vincent O'Sullivan who knew both Bosie and Wilde stated: 'It was even said that when the scandal began the police would have given him (OW) ample latitude to get out of England.' Why did he not go? The answer is complex. Oscar's mother, Lady Wilde, encouraged him to stay for the sake of the family's honour. For those who decree Bosie to be the agent of Wilde's fall, O'Sullivan counters: 'The opinion put forward that Wilde was a weak, flabby person, victimised by his friends should be abandoned. He was just the contrary; he was a force. Nobody in the wide world could persuade him to do what he did not want to do... he was certainly not the victim of his friends.' In a letter to Lord Alfred Douglas, the playwright summed up his feelings succinctly: 'A dishonoured name, a hunted life, are not for me.'

On April 19th, Oscar Wilde and Alfred Taylor were committed for trial at the Old Bailey. Lord Alfred Douglas contributed £50 towards Taylor's defence fund. Bosie maintained a prison vigil, visiting Wilde daily at Holloway prison; 'A slim thing, gold-haired like an angel stands always by my side' as Oscar would describe the scene in a letter to friends. When they were not together, Wilde and Douglas maintained a fervent correspondence, pledging vows of eternal loyalty. This would continue when Bosie was prevailed upon to leave the country by Oscar and his legal team. Many wanted to know why Lord Alfred Douglas had not been arrested and so on April 25th, 'ashen pale' as described by a witness, he departed for France. A foul glee erupted in England when both Oscar Wilde and Alfred Taylor were sentenced to two years hard labour for acts of gross indecency. Outside the Old Bailey, female prostitutes flashed their wares in jubilation, a couple of the 'panthers' were seen laughing as they jumped into a cab, whilst the newspapers did a venomous jig at the expense of a man whose work had once delighted the public;

'Open the windows, let in the fresh air!' trumpeted *The Daily Telegraph*. The dandy was dead. Beauty in art began to be eyed with suspicion and a return to hearty themes swiftly followed.

In exile, the scarlet butterfly was to find himself ostracised wherever he ventured. Whilst in Paris, Bosie was snubbed by a member of the royal family with whom he had previously enjoyed a cordial relationship. The scent of scandal was to follow him forever more. Staying in Le Havre, Douglas received anonymous notes warning him that he was under police surveillance after a local paper wrote derogatory comments on his decision to hire a boat with a small crew of sailors. He was also under the surveillance of the spirit world, his deceased maternal grandmother, Fanny Montgomery, sending a message at a séance attended by Lady Queensberry. Through a 'violently agitated' medium, Fanny warned that Bosie was 'surrounded by powerful enemies' and needed to get as far away as possible. He decamped for Sorrento, with his grandmother's ghostly assurance that he had 'good friends in the spirit world,' which was more than he had in the corporeal one.

With Apollo doing time in the big house, Bosie's poems became particularly melancholy and his exile, for all the pretty surroundings, was not an easeful one as 'The Travelling Companion' implies, 'I bent my eyes upon the summer land, And all the painted fields were ripe for me, And every flower nodded to my hand; But sorrow came and led me back to thee.' To fill the hours and with no heed of consequences – never his strong point – Douglas fired off letters in support of Oscar Wilde and homosexuality to a number of periodicals and their editors, often in response to torrents of invective against the imprisoned man. None of Wilde's other friends went out on the ledge in such a public manner at such a dangerous time, including Robbie Ross, who as a canny diplomat took a more obsequious route into Oscar's good books. Tact was not one of Bosie's strong points and he campaigned in a vociferous fashion, petitioning Queen Victoria to shorten Oscar's sentence as well as approaching a number of French writers in the hope that they would make a stand for Wilde.

The fact that Lord Alfred refused to halt his pen largely explains why he was never to be let back into royal circles after the scandal had died down. In August, 1895, on the behest of the

French magazine, *Mercure de France*, Douglas wrote a heartfelt feature that included in the summation; 'The incarceration of Oscar Wilde is a disgrace and an outrage on civilization. Liberty and Justice demand that he be released before the barbarities of the English prison system will have killed his body and destroyed his soul.' News of the article was, surprisingly, poorly received by Wilde, who asked that it not be published. The prison system, whilst not destroying Oscar's soul, had nonetheless contorted it via an unspeakably harsh regime. Unbeknownst to Bosie, another trinity had formed in which he was to reprise the role of temptation, with co-star Robbie Ross as the catalyst for far reaching disaster and Wilde, once again, the voice of conscience. It was Ross who had suggested that for Oscar's own good, Douglas should cease writing to him. Bosie acquiesced believing it was the right thing to do.

After Holloway Prison, Wilde had been transferred to Reading Gaol and it was here, in early February of 1896, that he received an unearthly visitation from his mother. He asked her to stay awhile in his cell but she mournfully demurred and vanished. The following day Constance came to see Oscar. A liberal who championed women's rights, Constance had carved a niche for herself as an esteemed public speaker but she had been crushed by the scandal and was now seriously ill with a spinal condition that caused gradual paralysis. This tragic illness reflected a threat included in the Golden Dawn's long ago pledge. The oath of secrecy about the teachings and rites of the order was enforced on 'pain of being paralysed without visible weapon.'

When the Wilde scandal broke, Constance Wilde had fled to Genoa with Cyril and Vyvyan. The woman of little importance valiantly dragged herself across continents because she could not bear the thought of her husband hearing the news of his mother's death from strangers. Wilde already knew the reason for Constance's visit and blamed himself for his mother's demise. He was in the depths, there was no place lower to go and in the shattered fragments of his life Oscar Wilde found a scarlet scapegoat and began to compose a letter to him that would become *De Profundis*. Wilde knew not why the angel who had once stood beside him in the gloom no longer wrote to him, of Ross's cruel intervention. In his cell, the image of a 'graceful boy with a Christ-like heart' began to metamorphose; oh Judas! Salome! Dorian! Douglas! He was all of the evils and more. As a therapeutic tool, *De Profundis* is unsurpassable but it took on the shape of a terrible wish that ultimately would be granted. Any work pored over in the deepest meditation and with the most intense emotions takes on a life of its own and once unleashed there is no way in which it can be reined in, much like a curse. Without question, *Dorian Gray* had a deleterious influence and now it was the turn of *De Profundis*. As always, Bosie was the recipient of Wilde's desire and the author expressed himself most eloquently in the letter's final lines: 'You came to me to learn the pleasure of life and the pleasure of art. Perhaps I am chosen to teach you something much more wonderful – the meaning of sorrow and it's beauty.' The true of extent of the horror would not be revealed to Lord Alfred Douglas for a further 17 years; a letter from a dead man's hand. However, the mystery remains whether Wilde wished Bosie to read the missive. He seems to have left it to the fates to decide when, on his release from prison, on May 19th, 1897, he handed the manuscript to Robbie Ross.

The French have an expression for it: 'Amour Fou' – crazy love – the English of course do not. Robbie Ross, Constance Wilde and Lord & Lady Queensberry had many other words for the reunion of Oscar Wilde and Lord Alfred Douglas in Rouen on August 28th, 1897. Ross and Constance now had the bankrupt Wilde on a stipend, doling out expenses whilst Sybil had put her son on an £8 a week allowance. Oscar began playing Douglas off Ross, because he knew Robbie would cough up the pennies for the vicarious thrill of having him tarnish the golden boy. Vincent O'Sullivan noted of Robbie's financial ministrations that: 'Ross persuaded people that all sums destined for Oscar should pass through his hands. Wilde would say with a sigh 'Robbie is a dear, but does not understand'. He preferred that any money he received outside the Ross administration should not be mentioned to Ross. Unsurprisingly, Robbie was 'extremely angry' according to writer, Hesketh Pearson, when he heard of the meeting in Rouen. If *De Profundis* really held true then Wilde would never have resumed relations with Lord Alfred, nor would they have planned to go to Naples together, later in the year. 'My going back to Bosie was psychologically inevitable,' Oscar would write to Robbie, 'I cannot live without the atmosphere of love. Of course I shall often be unhappy, but I still love him, the mere fact that he wrecked my life makes me love him.' Though Douglas had not yet done jail-time, he could equally have said the same.

History is littered with destructive, alchemical relationships where the ruin of the lovers is passion's privilege. In society's eyes, both men were pariahs. Even amongst Wilde's coterie, there was now a view held by some that the playwright was jinxed as Vincent O'Sullivan posited, 'The notion that he (OW) brought bad luck was held by several. Beardsley had it so strongly that he would not keep even a book of Wilde's by him. None of those among his close friends seems to have had a fortunate life. Equally strange, and remarked by (OW) himself, is the fact that many died within a few years after he was cast into prison, or fell on misfortune in one shape or another.' Lord Alfred, whose name means 'Wise as a supernatural being' wasn't faring much better. Unfortunately, he wasn't very wise in anything save for poetry, and the supernatural is another matter. In the late summer of 1897, Vincent O'Sullivan received a letter from Wilde asking if they could meet in Paris. The missive was sent from Berneval on the French coast, where Ross had instated Wilde in a chalet, out of harm's way. Wilde wasn't having any of it. Over lunch in Montmartre, he confessed to O'Sullivan that his friends and family wanted him to go to a mountain village to write. Of this unbearably dismal prospect, O'Sullivan observed; 'What he (OW) required was to be stimulated, distracted from his black thoughts. How could he find that in a mountain village? It would have continued the penal cell. He himself was inclined to go to Italy.' Oscar's spiel was leading to the point that Lord Alfred Douglas awaited him in Italy but Wilde was flat broke. The kindly O'Sullivan gave him the necessary money, later commenting, 'It is not every day that one had the chance of relieving the anxiety of a genius and a hero. I think he left Paris the same evening.'

Oscar Wilde and Lord Alfred Douglas enjoyed a two-week break at the splendid Hotel Royal in Naples where they ran up a massive bill. Neither man could pay but the hotel never queried them until the very last, simply because they had an aristocrat in their midst. Without a penny in his pocket, Douglas was still able to give the impression of being swish. Next they moved to the charming Villa Giudice at Posilipo, with a sea view and four members of staff, including the helpful Michele. Despite the villa's pleasant appearance, they were to discover that it was over-run by rats. The rodents terrified Douglas who slept in a house across the street until they found a solution of which he observed:

'After a time, however, we got rid of the rats, partly by means of a professional and orthodox rat-catcher, but also (and chiefly, according to Oscar's opinion) owing to the ministrations, hired for a small fee, of a potent witch who was recommended as infallible by Michele, and who came and "burned odours" and muttered incantations which she assured us no rats could resist. She also told both our fortunes, and Oscar professed to regard her as a wonderful and powerful sorceress. In appearance she was quite the witch of literature and drama. She had a distinct beard and "with age and envy was grown into a hoop." Anyhow, the rats disappeared.'

The notion that Bosie was not Wilde's muse can be laid to rest in Naples. 'I feel my only hope of again doing beautiful work in art is being with you,' he had written to Lord Alfred shorty before their Italian sojourn. One can imagine them on the terrace in Naples, overlooking the ocean, Oscar completing 'The Ballad of Reading Gaol' whilst Bosie who had matured in both spirit and literary style, composed sonnets. Lord Alfred's poetry had a sparse elegance, unlike the ornate transcendence that Wilde was at times prone to. In that sense, Oscar was a sorcerer, his work striving to go beyond mortal realms. Lord Alfred Douglas could never have written *Dorian Gray* but nor could Wilde have composed with Bosie's slender measure. It was in Naples that Douglas wrote the breath-taking 'City of The Soul' realising all too well that their beautiful retreat was about to be stormed...

'And every passing moment is a bell,
To mourn the death of undiscerned delight.
Where is the sun that made the noon-day bright,
And where the midnight moon? O let us tell,

In long carved line and painted parable,
How the white road curves down into the night.

Only to build one crystal barrier
Against this sea which beats upon our days;
To ransom one lost moment with a rhyme
Of passionate protest or austere demur,
To clutch Life's hair, and thrust one naked phrase
Like a lean knife between the ribs of Time.'

Photographs of the pair taken in Naples reveal a rather pinched aspect to Bosie's fine features whilst linear shadows like prison bars dapple Oscar's linen jacket. He may have been free but he was bound by conditions as was Lord Alfred Douglas. By the autumn of 1897, the dream of the two men being able to live together was fading fast due to the vehement machinations of others, the hand of Robbie Ross at the wheel once again. However, the 'crystal barrier' was initially breached when the local papers reported that Douglas and Wilde were cohabiting. They were subsequently visited by Beauchamp Denis Browne, an attaché from the British Embassy who warned them that the arrangement was undesirable. Ironically, Giudice, the name of the Villa, stems from 'judge' or 'justice' and their personal liberty was again imperilled. The incident gave further credence to Ross, Constance and Lady Queensberry who were all united in their condemnation of Wilde and Douglas having taken up again.

Robbie Ross actively encouraged Constance Wilde, who now referred to Douglas as the 'BEAST' to cut off her husband's allowance. He also wrote to publisher Leonard Smithers, who hoped to issue 'The Ballad of Reading Gaol' to inform him that the work had no value and that he should desist from paying Wilde. He was effectively attempting to starve them out. And he succeeded. All they now had to live on was Bosie's allowance but in December, Lady Queensberry notified her son that if he didn't leave Wilde she would cut him off. Seeing no other option, Lord Alfred agreed but fought to give Wilde back his financial dignity with a series of conditions that included covering the rent on the villa for a further three months and a generous payment of £200. As Sybil saw it, the sums were a small price for her son's soul. Vincent O'Sullivan met with a down-cast Wilde in Naples, shortly after Bosie's departure, recalling 'He (OW) pointed out to me in the street an old woman. "Unless that old woman asks you for money do not offer it to her. But if she asks you, be sure not to refuse." Some days later we were sitting in a restaurant when the witch came by. She paused for a moment, looked at us both steadfastly, and then went her way. Wilde was very much disturbed. "Did you see that? She has looked in at the window. Some great misfortune is going to happen to us."'

On April 7th, 1898, Constance Wilde died following complications from an operation. Wilde, now living in Paris, dreamt of the once 'violet-eyed Artemis' that same night. Though Constance had tried to curb Wilde's relationship with Lord Alfred Douglas by financial constraint, she had been used as an unwitting pawn. Ross had put pressure on Wilde to slur Douglas and he had acquiesced, writing a letter in which he claimed that Bosie had lived royally off him in Naples and did nothing to chip in... 'When it came to his (Bosie) having to pay his own share he became terrible, unkind, mean and penurious, except where his own pleasures were concerned, and when my allowance ceased, he left...' It is pitiful to think of Wilde having to appease Ross, who showed the letter to Constance. How bitter were the seasonings of the whole unhappy saga. Efficient as ever, the forward thinking Ross stored Wilde's Naples letter alongside *De Profundis*. Though Oscar and Lord Alfred saw each other less frequently, they nonetheless remained in contact and when Bosie took an apartment on Avenue Kleber, Wilde helped him to choose the furniture. On one occasion they celebrated the issue of Bosie's anonymously published book *The City of The Soul* together, drinking to the unknown poet, for both of their names were still synonymous with scandal. The spell had been broken after Naples, Douglas writing to his mother 'I am tired of the struggle and tired of being ill-treated by the World and I had lost that supreme desire for his (OW's) society which I had before and which made a sort of aching void when he was not with me. That had gone and I think and hope for ever.' The fever had abated but not the friendship.

Like sombre book-ends, the deaths of Queensberry and Oscar Wilde began and concluded 1900. John Sholto Douglas, who had gnawed on his hat during Wilde's trial, remained irrational to the last, suffering delusions that the 'Oscar Wilders' were after him in his final days. Learning that his father was unwell, Bosie went to visit him at Bailey's Hotel in Kensington, where Queensberry shed reconciliatory tears and promised to reinstate his darling boy's allowance. When the sobbing subsided, Queensberry dashed off an abusive letter to his son retracting the offer. After a death-bed confessional, The Eighth Marquis of Queensberry was received into the Catholic Church and died on January 31st, 1900, having forgotten to cut Bosie out of his will. Lacking financial common sense and little realising that he could have lived comfortably off the interest generated by his £15,000 inheritance, Lord Alfred Douglas dashed through his cash on horses, the race-track and business follies, not to mention wining and dining Oscar in Paris. Bosie was out of the country when news reached him that Wilde was ailing though his rapid deterioration due to meningitis could not have been anticipated. One famous story about Oscar's final hours is recalled by Vincent O'Sullivan; 'As he (OW) lay dying, a friend of his, known in London for his witty sayings, came over to see him and was sitting with him. Wilde awoke from a doze and said; 'I have had an appalling dream. I dreamed I was banqueting with the dead.' 'My dear Oscar,' replied the other cheerfully, 'I am sure you were the life and soul of the party.'

Oscar Wilde died on November 30th, 1900, at the age of forty-six. To his deepest chagrin, Bosie arrived too late to say goodbye and agreed to pay for the funeral. Throughout the baleful proceedings Robert Ross remained the epitome of efficiency; one requires clarity at times of crisis and Bosie who led the mourners was distracted by grief. Douglas had always let his emotions get the better of him, but Ross was there, calming hand at the wheel, as Caspar Winterman's explains in *A Poet's Life and his Work*: 'Ross then said he had looked at the deceased's papers, without finding anything of importance. What should be done with these? Should he (Ross) take care of them? Bosie's head was in a whirl. He answered that Ross should do what he thought best. As a result, Ross had been appointed de facto Oscar's literary executor, having at his disposal not only the manuscript of *De Profundis* but also a sheaf of letters from Bosie to Oscar.' Now it is true that in the years to come, Robbie Ross did a wonderful job of restoring Wilde's work and reputation in a way that the impetuous Douglas could probably not have managed. Ross and Douglas were direct opposites, control set against impulse.

It is a great pity that after Wilde's death, no one gently led Bosie away to a nice ivory tower where he could have spent his days doing what he did best: writing poetry. He should have been kept as far away from real life as possible. Though not as superstitious as Oscar Wilde, one poem, 'Palmistry,' touches upon Bosie's uncertain future after the playwright's demise. It also features a reoccurring theme in his work, that of the soul trapped beneath the skin, longing to be free, 'The sleeper stirred And softly moaned; and, prisoned in a mesh, Methought I saw his soul, a frightened bird, Behind the eternal barriers of flesh. At length his body quickened with slow sighs And broke the bondage of his sleeping-pace. He turned his head and opened wide his eyes. And looked at me – and lo! Twas mine own face.'

Penniless, Bosie followed in the gigolo shoes of Lord Reggie Hastings, travelling to the US in the hope of bagging an American heiress but his scarlet reputation scuppered his chances. Despite gaining honorary membership of the prestigious Metropolitan club in Washington, he was asked to leave because of his 'doings with objectionable persons in London.' Unfortunately, the press also got hold of the story. Of his many detractors, Douglas would write: 'I mentally assigned them to the devil, who by the way, appears to have taken me at my word in a good many cases.' However, Douglas had already become embroiled with a Colonel's daughter, Olive Custance, who whilst having a reasonable income wasn't minted, but love won out in the end. Olive was a poet and literary groupie who had enjoyed a liaison with the American writer, Nathalie Barney. Of their trip to Venice, Caspar Winterman's writes, 'Olive hung a photograph of a statue of Antinous in her hotel room, saying to Natalie that the favourite of the Emperor Hadrian, who had proclaimed him a god after his untimely death, reminded her of Alfred Douglas. On him she had bestowed her heart.' Olive married Antinous on March 4th, 1902, in a secret ceremony, breaking the news to her parent's later. Sybil raised no objections, perhaps believing that her son's soul was finally out of danger. Keeping Douglas in his sights, Robbie Ross attended the wedding. It wasn't one of those 'Should have been me' moments, rather it was a case of 'it should have been Oscar' according to Douglas Murray in his book *Bosie* who observed: 'From the back of the church Robert Ross watched as the lover of his greatest friend, the golden Adonis and fated love of Oscar Wilde, married a woman in a Christian ceremony celebrating their love. Douglas had found a love that spoke its name and had a right to do so in the eyes of the law as well as in the eyes of society. As he sat and brooded, Ross took in a scene he would never forget and which he could not forgive.' On November 17th, Lady Olive Douglas gave birth to Bosie's sole heir, Raymond Wilfrid Sholto, described as 'an attractive, affectionate, child, healthy but highly strung.' The family moved into a delightful old property, 'Lake Farm' near the river Avon, and enjoyed an idyllic, rural life, although Colonel Custance was a little possessive of Raymond, having always longed for a son.

No matter how he played it, Lord Alfred Douglas possessed a lethal gift for offending all sides; some felt he had sold out homosexuality, most heterosexuals treated him with suspicion until the end of his life, and everyone queries bi-sexuality, which he bravely admitted to in 1929, proclaiming: 'I believe that almost everyone is more or less bisexual.' In this stance, he anticipated pop culture and was to be portrayed by Marianne Faithfull who played 'Bosie' to Mick Jagger's pouting 'Wilde' in a short film to promote the Rolling Stone's song, 'We Love You.' With Keith Richard's in the role of the judge, the early video, made in 1968, pastiches Wilde's trail, complete with carnations in a vase. The film is a pointed reference to a drug bust at Keith Richard's house, where Marianne Faithfull was daubed a scarlet woman after it was revealed she was found naked under a rug when the police raided the property. At the time, Faithfull was reading 'The Great God Pan' by former Golden Dawn initiate, Arthur Machen.

It would seem that Bosie's scarlet spirit was still infectious and so unfortunately was the century's old Queensberry curse. Though now hailed as one of the greatest fantasy writers of his generation, Arthur Machen, like many other cash-strapped authors dipped his pen into journalism and started contributing features – under the editorship of Lord Alfred Douglas – to a newspaper called *The Academy*. Suffering the same financial duress as Machen, Lord Alfred could not survive on poetry alone and had gladly taken the post of editor. Former members of the

Wilde coterie, including the ubiquitous Robbie Ross and Reggie Turner would also produce articles for *The Academy* in its early days. Ross, meanwhile, had been busy as Wilde's 'literary executor.' In 1905, Robbie had overseen the publication of a highly expurgated edition of *De Profundis* in which it was insinuated that he was the intended recipient of the letter. Douglas, none the wiser, reviewed it, stating: 'The trace of the master is still visible' but it 'certainly cannot rank with measurable distance of his best work.' The book, clumsily abridged by Ross, wasn't a good representation of Wilde but Bosie's review intensified an already simmering situation and Robbie reacted badly. This time, the fight was out in the open. In his *Bosie* book, Rupert Croft-Cooke recalls a heated scene between the two men, noting, 'Bosie was furious when Ross refused to show him the manuscript. He abused Ross who said "If you talk to me like that I'll publish the manuscript and that will finish you off."'

As the magical years spent with Wilde receded, Lord Alfred gradually assumed the belligerent Queensberry style, using his newspaper as a platform from which to vent often bigoted opinions on politics and religion and by becoming increasingly litigious as well as homophobic. A martyr to the madness of his bloodline, he had wandered too far from the ivory tower and the only place where his soul now sang undimmed was in poetry. The sorrowful 'Stones for Bread' echoes down the years back to Oscar, with its reference to Asphodels, an everlasting flower that grows in the Elysian fields of Greek mythology... 'Ah woe to us who look for asphodel Where asphodel is not, and bitter woe To us who bid the barren gardens blow With fabulous flowers; who hear the silver bell Chiming from some enchanted citadel, When flower and bell and citadel lie low in the lost dust of dreams. Naked we know, Through fire and ice, the fall from Heaven to Hell.' The elegy recalls Wilde's poem 'Athanasia,' which includes a verse particularly applicable to Douglas... 'Ah no! to this bright flower a thousand years Seemed but the lingering of a summer's day. It never knew the tide of cankering fears Which turns a boy's gold hair to withered grey.' Whilst still editor of *The Academy*, a correspondence ensued between Douglas and the playwright, George Bernard Shaw, after he received a scathing review in the paper. Although the two would later become friends, Shaw accused Bosie of drunkenness, which the former Hyacinthus flatly denied. Worse however was Shaw's pertinent observation of the disparities in Bosie's character; 'There are two Douglases – A.D the poet and – shall I say? – the hereditary Douglas.' Shaw's letter concludes tellingly...'That hereditary Douglas, when he gets loose from A.D, is capable of wrecking a paper – even of wrecking himself.' In this, Lord Alfred was to get ample help and not just from himself.

To the left and to the right, former members of the Golden Dawn were assembling. The most famous of all the initiates of the order was Aleister Crowley, and now he stepped up with cloven hooves. The self-appointed 'Wickedest Man In the World,' a.k.a. 'The Beast 666,' was – surprisingly for one who revelled in scandal and also bisexual – not a fan of Lord Alfred Douglas, whose conversion to Catholicism soured the scarlet, at least from Crowley's perspective. The 'Beast's' contribution to Bosie's eldritch legacy commenced with a poem entitled 'A Slim Gilt Soul' that includes the following verse:

> 'For what were lovelier on the lawn
> Than you, pearl-naked to the dawn,
> Wrapped in a scarlet dressing-gown
> Not thirty miles from London town,
> The "observed of all observers" – save
> That Scotland Yard, serene and suave,
> When trouble came, went tramping by;
> Closed one, and winked the other eye.
> How pleasantly you must have smiled;
> "I left them and I left them wild."'

'The Great Beast' also produced 'The Child' an equally inflammatory acrostic poem that bears Lord Alfred's name in the text, as part of a sustained literary attack in which he hoped to draw Bosie out into a court-room scrap but Aleister was to be disappointed. On advice, Douglas demurred the Beast's baiting. However, Crowley would return at the lowest ebb of Bosie's life, three years later, in time for the book of revelations, a.k.a. *De Profundis* to be fully served on Lord Alfred Douglas in a court of law. It was then that Wilde's invocation to Douglas, that he should learn 'the meaning of sorrow and its beauty' assumed full effect. The catalyst was Robbie Ross.

'All trials are trials for one's life, just as all sentences are sentences of death' Wilde gravely pronounced in *De Profundis*. Now it was Oscar's turn to pass literary sentence, and Lord Alfred Douglas would become one of the most reviled men in history as a consequence. But the question remains, would Wilde have wanted *De Profundis* to be let loose on his former amour? Responsibility had never been Oscar's strong point, and he left it to Robbie Ross to act as fate's emissary but not without prompting. Never underestimate the significance of dates: On April 1st, 1897, a month before his release from Reading Gaol, Wilde had written to Robbie with directives on the manuscript: 'Someday the truth will have to be known – not necessarily in my lifetime... but I am not prepared to sit in the grotesque gallery they put me into, for all time; for the simple reason that I inherited from my father and my mother a name of high distinction in literature and art, and I cannot for eternity allow that name to be degraded. I do not defend my conduct. I explain it...' Oscar also left instructions on how the letter should be copied and then delivered in the manner of a papal decree. After 1535, the seal on such decrees was decorated with Fleur De Lys, as Wilde, the most learned of men must surely have known. In 'De Profundis,' Wilde mentions that Bosie had adopted the name 'Prince Fleur De Lys' which he used in correspondence to Oscar when he was first incarcerated. Now it was time for the seal to be pulled apart. In 1909, Ross had given *De Profundis* to the British Museum with the instructions that it shouldn't be opened until 60 years had passed, by which time everyone involved would be as incense on the breeze, memory's dusty plumes. However, a nascent Oscar Wilde industry was gathering speed, the backbone of which was biographical. In 1910, the publisher Martin Secker commissioned a young author called Arthur Ransome, to write a book on Oscar Wilde. At the beginning of his career and less astute than a more seasoned biographer, Arthur was initially grateful for the invaluable input that Robbie Ross gave him, including a copy of *De Profundis* and the 'forsaken in Naples' missive. Ross would deny having provided anything that related to Douglas, a claim that Ransome later refuted in his memoirs. Unwittingly, the inexperienced Arthur Ransome had been pulled into a scarlet web. When *Oscar Wilde; A Critical Study* was published on February 16th, 1912, Bosie was perplexed.

Though not referring to Lord Alfred Douglas directly, Ransome related a litany of charges to 'The friendship'...that had 'already cost (OW) more than it was worth, whose conduct he had condemned, whose influence he had feared' and who had left him wrung out in Naples. Seeking clarity, Lord Alfred Douglas wrote to Robbie Ross, wanting to know exactly to whom *De Profundis* was addressed and pointing out: 'Anyone reading the book carefully with a full knowledge of the circumstances would be led to infer that I was the "friend" referred to.' If Ross had conspired to hurt Lord Alfred Douglas by putting him on trial for his reputation, in the way that Wilde had been, he succeeded. Wasn't it an encyclical decree that Wilde had demanded in his *De Profundis* directive to Ross? What goes around, comes around. As Ross probably anticipated, Douglas acted in his usual impassioned manner and made the decision to sue both the publisher and the author. However, it wasn't damages that he was seeking, despite having just been declared bankrupt, but to clear his name. The ever thoughtful Ross offered to pay for the defence's legal team, which aroused Martin Secker's suspicion that Wilde's executor was playing a long dreadful game at Bosie's expense. Although Secker would apologise to Lord Alfred Douglas, it was now too late to turn back. The trial opened on April 17th, Douglas going into battle with substandard legal representation due to his penurious finances. Judge Darling, a known homophobe whose poetry had not been well received in *The Academy*, was hardly impartial to try the case. It was to be a public blood-bath for Lord Alfred Douglas whose name was once again splashed in scarlet by the press. In a scene mirroring Wilde's trail and the domination of *Dorian Gray*, pages of *De Profundis* were read out in court, the terrible intensity of Wilde's judgement upon Bosie for all to hear. At one point during proceedings, the dazed Lord Alfred wandered off, absenting himself because he wanted to believe that he didn't have to be present for the annihilation. Escorted back into court, Darling publically admonished Douglas. With his usual efficiency Ross had carried out his role as executor to the final full stop, Wilde's closing lines to Bosie in *De Profundis* – 'Perhaps I am chosen to teach you something much more wonderful – the meaning of sorrow and its beauty', having hit the mark as surely as a slim gilt arrow. But it was also Oscar Wilde who wrote in the 'Ballad of Reading Gaol': 'Each man kills the thing he loves, yet each man does not die,' those very words polished to glittering brilliance in Bosie's company, over-looking the sea in Naples. Douglas did not perish, but he was done for. Running virtually concurrent to the Douglas versus Ransome case, Colonel Custance had fought for custody of his grandson and won. Penniless, Olive had also been manipulated into leaving her husband by the Colonel. The Ransome court-case would only have strengthened the argument.

Joining the ravening mob of public opinion against Douglas following the Ransome trial, 'The Beast, 666' in conjunction with society hostess, Elizabeth Gwendoline Otter, produced an anti-Bosie pamphlet *The Writing On The Ground*. When Douglas again failed to react, Crowley dashed off an offensive essay entitled 'The Writing on The Wall' that proclaimed: '"Bosie" is a common prostitute, blackmailer, sodomite, and my name is Aleister Crowley, and my address is 33 Avenue Studios, London S.W.' Yet again, Crowley was to be thwarted by Bosie's indifference though he does mention a leaflet called 'The Writing on The Floor' in *Oscar Wilde and Myself* which is described as 'malice and wicked propaganda.' Unlike Crowley, who was out of the starting gate as fast his cloven hooves would take him in condemning Bosie, another former member of The Golden Dawn, Arthur Machen, held off until February 4th, 1921 when he wrote an obituary of Lord Alfred Douglas that appeared in *The Evening News*. According to the slender epitaph, Lord Alfred had died suddenly, from 'Heart failure after a chill,' having worked late into the night on his weekly journal *Plain English*. Once again, Lord Alfred Douglas was back in the news and in the most unhappiest of circumstances. Under the headline 'A Great Life Spoilt – How the Evil Genius of the Douglasses dogged Lord Alfred,' Machen summarised Bosie's deeds, 'A brilliant and most unhappy career is ended. Lord Alfred Douglas was born, in a sense, under the happiest of auspices. He was a Douglas, the son of one of the most ancient families in Great Britain. He was connected with many of the "best people" in society, he had brilliant capacities, and showed that he was certainly to be numbered amongst the poets. He might have done anything and his poetry excepted, he did nothing and worse than nothing. That charity which is fitting at all times, but most fitting when we are speaking of the newly dead, urges that much should be forgiven this poor, bewildered man who with all this gifts, will perhaps only be remembered by the scandals and the quarrels in which he involved himself.' Machen with his supreme understanding of the supernatural, which he employed in his best stories, concluded the obituary on a salient, if cautionary note; 'It is a great thing... to be born a Douglas but the family inheritance has gifts from evil fairies as well as good ones... many of them were violently eccentric; to put the case mildly.'

A troubled soul in this life and the next, Lord Alfred Douglas lived a further 24 years after the obituary was published, finally escaping the impenetrable confines of flesh on March 20th, 1945, having borne witness to the long terrible fade of everything he had held dear. Though separated, Douglas was to remain friends with Olive and was inconsolable that she died without having fully converted to Catholicism. Their son, Raymond, a schizophrenic, was to spend the majority of his life confined to an institution. 'Beyond the stars, could but its silver bell outchime the iron knell of miscalled doom, How would not Death come kindly with mild eyes?' (*Oxford Revisited*, 1932) No one had desired death more keenly than Lord Alfred Douglas and his wish was finally granted. But his repose is not a quiet one and the terrible beating wings of 'The Queensberry Curse' is still very much active, at least according to an article that appeared in *The Daily Express* in August 2009, which was prefaced by the lead-in headline; 'Lord Milo Douglas who threw himself to his death from a tower block was the latest member of a troubled aristocratic family with a chequered history.' The feature continues:

'On a rainy night last month a 34 year-old charity worker named Milo Douglas climbed to the top of a block of council flats in central London and jumped off... Milo, a teacher turned outreach worker was the third son of the 12th Marquis of Queensberry. It was the saddest of endings to a life that had long been troubled by manic depression – and only the latest incident in a trail of tragedy visited upon one of the oldest families in the land... he is the victim of what might be termed the Queensberry curse, an affliction that has seen family members meet untimely ends. In life they have forged alliances which are unconventional to say the least. The current generation of the extended Douglas clan includes a former bank robber and a brother of the world's most wanted man, Osama Bin Laden.'

BOSIE AND THE BEAST

'Wait and watch and watch and wait,
He shall pay the half and the whole,
Now or then, or soon or late,
(Steel or lead or hempen cord,
And the devil take his soul!)'

A Ballad of Hate
– Lord Alfred Douglas, September 1894

Each century has its spirits of disturbance, those beings whose actions affect the very fabric of society either by default or design. In the case of Lord Alfred Douglas, an impassioned mutual attachment with Oscar Wilde created a maelstrom. However, Douglas did not consciously pursue controversy. A man of unguarded passions, Lord Alfred came from an ancient if aristocratic lineage descended from blood-thirsty Scottish chieftains and blighted with instability; 'The mad, bad line' as Oscar Wilde once referred to the Douglas clan, who at the time were presided over by the fearsome John Sholto Douglas, the eighth Marquess of Queensberry. His title alone would have guaranteed Lord Alfred social renown unlike his shadowy bête noire Aleister Crowley, who of less eminent birth-right, had to create his own mythology as 'The Great Beast, 666' a.k.a. 'The Wickedest Man In The World.' No one worked harder for infamy's crown than Crowley yet Douglas hardly had to break a sweat to utterly annihilate his own reputation whilst being universally condemned for ruining Oscar Wilde and all before turning twentyfive. In the spring of 1895, when Wilde was put on trial and crucified in the dock for homosexuality, Lord Alfred was cast in the role of temptation, forever taking his place in history. Amongst the Douglas related evidence used against Wilde was the 'Red Rose-Leaf' letter which commences:

'My own Boy,
Your sonnet is quite lovely, and it is a marvel that those red rose-leaf lips of yours should have been made no less for music of song than for madness of kisses. Your slim gilt soul walks between passion and poetry. I know Hyacinthus, whom Apollo loved so madly, was you in Greek days...
Always with undying love
Yours
Oscar'

Aleister Crowley would later turn at least some of the 'Red Rose-Leaf' contents against L.A.D, trying him through literary means. Though now regarded as Wilde's 'Homme Fatale,' Douglas was not the lone component that brought about the playwright's imprisonment on charges of gross indecency – a legal immolation that showed both justice and Britain at its very worst. The terrible series of events that led to Oscar Wilde's trial is too complex for easy deduction, at least for the purpose of this essay, but it placed Bosie in the spotlight as a scapegoat. Following Wilde's incarceration, Lord Alfred Douglas was socially ostracised, deemed the masculine equivalent of a scarlet woman. At this time, the occultist – a hostile observer – sharpened his claws. What is surprising about Aleister Crowley's particularly virulent attacks upon Lord Alfred is his unusual readiness to align himself with public opinion. Crowley after all loathed convention, venerated intrigue, and had relationships with both men and women. In his excellent book *Alfred Douglas – A Poet's Life and His Finest Work*, biographer Caspar Wintermans succinctly notes: 'Envy! One cannot wholly rid oneself of the impression that the mud which over the years has been slung at Lord Alfred derives in part, consciously or unconsciously, from this feeling. After all, most of us aren't really beautiful. Most of us are not of noble birth. Most of us are not so charming as to be capable of charming charming people like Oscar Wilde – if we ever meet them that is. And then we cannot write poetry – at least not as well as to gain the praise of masters like Stéphane Mallarmé. Bosie was extremely privileged. That irked and continues to irk.'

Although my favourite of Aleister Crowley's aliases has always been Little Sunshine – produced during a 1934 libel case

–he was usually prone to loftier titles, assuming at different times the aliases of Laird Boleskine, Lord Boleskine and Lord Lockey. Crowley's predilection for pseudonyms probably dates back to childhood, when his mother, inspired by the *Book of Revelations*, bestowed upon him the soubriquet of 'The Beast'; Lord Alfred had to make do with the rather less imposing pet name of 'Bosie'. Only five years in age separates the two; Lord Alfred having arrived via gilded stork on October 22nd, 1870 whilst Aleister descended upon Warwickshire on October 12th, 1875, later commenting 'It has been remarked a strange coincidence that one small county should have given England her two greatest poets' – this of course is not a reference to Bosie who alighted in Worcester, home of the sauce, but to Shakespeare. The early flowering of both Aleister and Alfred's poetic talents bloomed whilst at university. Douglas being the elder was always one dainty leap ahead, entering Magdalen College, Oxford, in 1889.

Making up for a fragrantly lackadaisical approach to his studies, Bosie drew praise for a melancholy poem, 'Autumn Days,' which was published in *The Oxford Magazine*. The lilt of regret that runs through 'Autumn Days' is at odds with the daring and frivolous image of Douglas as a young man and could be considered a prelude to the catastrophe that was to follow. The stage was set in the summer of 1891, when the poet Lionel Johnson introduced Lord Alfred Douglas to Oscar Wilde and a love missile was unwittingly aimed at polite society. It would take four years to detonate creating the greatest scandal of fin de siè-cle England and decimating Wilde and Douglas in the process. But foresight – much like hindsight – is the tidy province of casual bystanders and historians. Oscar Wilde, married with children and approaching middle age, became infatuated by Bosie, who at nineteen possessed a 'flower-like' beauty (according to George Bernard Shaw) and thus commenced one of the most complex liaisons of all time. The relationship bore elements of co-dependency, being both rapturous and fraught, not to mention dangerous as to be homosexual made them sexual outlaws. Douglas was needy, Wilde besotted, reconciliations inevitably followed rows, but the poetry was unsurpassable, the love letters sublime, and Wilde's plays hugely successful. The highs were greater than heaven and the lows more desolate than the grave. Under Wilde's spell, Lord Alfred emerged as one of the most promising poets of the age, although his university education went up in a blaze of blackmail threats and red rose leaves.

In December 1894, *The Chameleon*, a student magazine started by John Francis Bloxam that promised 'A bazaar of dangerous and smiling chances,' published 'Two Loves' and 'In Praise of Shame,' by Lord Alfred Douglas, which were to be raked over at Wilde's trial. In the latter, Bosie employed a lyrical symbolism, in which 'shame' – an allusion to homosexuality – is exalted. In this he was utterly fearless as 'In Praise of Shame' demonstrates:

> 'Last night unto my bed methought there came
> Our lady of strange dreams, and from an urn
> She poured live fire, so that mine eyes did burn
> At sight of it. Anon the floating flame
> Too many shapes, and one cried: "I am Shame
> That walks with Love, I am most wise to turn
> Cold lips and limbs to fire; therefore discern
> And see my loveliness, and praise my name."
>
> And afterwards, in radiant garments dressed
> With sound of flutes and laughing of glad lips,
> A pomp of all the passions passed along
> All the night through; till the white phantom ships
> Of dawn sailed in. Whereat I said this song,
> "Of all sweet passions Shame is loveliest."'

In the year of Wilde's trial, Aleister Crowley entered Trinity College, Cambridge. Certain aspects of Crowley's university life – occult awakenings aside – bear a similarity to those of another poet. Whilst at Trinity College, Crowley embarked on a relationship with an older man, Herbert Charles Jerome Pollitt, who introduced him to the world of decadent literature and influenced his poetic craft. A friend of Aubrey Beardsley and a keen art collector, Pollitt also performed female roles, including that of 'Diane D'Rougy' at Cambridge's Footlight Club. They enjoyed a passionate affair during which Crowley dashed off several poems praising shame, including 'The Ballad of Passive Pederasty':

'Of man's delight and man's desire
In one thing is no weariness –
To feel the fury of the fire,
And writhe within the close caress
Of fierce embrace, and wanton kiss
And final nuptial done aright,
How sweet a passion, shame, is this....'

During his courtship with Pollitt, Aleister Crowley also penned a scathing offensive against a Cambridge homosexual who supported Wilde's cause, which was issued in 'Mysteries, Lyrical and Dramatic.' (1898) There was an unexpected incongruity in Crowley's feelings towards Wilde. The Beast's ambivalence to Wilde is adroitly summarised by Timothy D'Arch Smith in the pamphlet, *Bunbury*, in which he explains: 'Crowley was not wholeheartedly in favour of Oscar Wilde. He found his behaviour snobbish, his writings second-rate and his amatory alignment fraudulently irresponsible in that Wilde failed to grasp the enormous, if limited, on occasion dangerous, spiritual forces to which he was exposed. He particularly objected to Wilde's addiction to irrumation which, in magical terms, he condemned as vampiric. Parallel, however, to this disapproval – the fact, doctrinally, that Wilde disobeyed his True Will – ran Crowley's abhorrence of British hypocrisy which had led to Wilde's downfall....' Aleister Crowley was to find himself on the fringes of the Wilde coterie, courtesy of Pollitt who introduced him to Oscar's publisher, Leonard Smithers. The association not only provided a home for his poetry, under the title of *White Stains*, but as part of a literary milieu, Crowley also became privy to certain anti-Bosie inferences.

White Stains was issued in a limited edition of 100 copies in May 1898. Exactly one year later, in May 1899, Lord Alfred's second collection of poetry *The City of The Soul* was published. Neither *White Stains* due to its contents or *The City of The Soul* because of Lord Alfred Douglas' reputation bore the name of the author, Crowley plumbing for a pseudonym, George Archibald Bishop, whilst Douglas settled on the more classic 'anonymous.' It is unlikely that Aleister Crowley rejoiced in the publication of *White Stains* with Pollitt as by then they had gone their separate ways. To Crowley's regret, Pollitt had no interest in the Magickal

Zeus & Ganymede/Apollo & Hyacinthus/Oscar & Bosie

workings that he had begun to pursue, having been initiated into the Golden Dawn. Bosie, however, celebrated the publication of *The City of The Soul* in the company of Oscar Wilde, their glasses tilted to the stars under the Parisian night.

One of the great mysteries to 'Bosie Bashers' (a term devised by Lord Alfred Douglas biographer Caspar Wintermans) has always been the continuation of relations between Oscar Wilde and Lord Alfred after the playwright was released from prison. Perhaps Wilde's words 'I cannot live without you' sent to Bosie in a note might in some way explain this. Their reunion overrides the scourging tones Wilde employed in his prison letter *De Profundis* to Bosie. Written in Reading Gaol, in the most dreadful conditions, Wilde was under the misconception that his 'graceful boy with a Christ-like heart' had abandoned him and did not hold back.

De Profundis, sadly, was to prove the whammy from beyond the grave but that was as yet to come. A distraught Bosie led the mourners at Wilde's funeral on December 3rd, 1900, at Bagneux on the outskirts of Paris. How bleak the thought of one of life's most extravagant peacocks being interred in a paupers grave. Douglas, in a letter to his friend More Adey, would write 'I am miserable and wretched about darling Oscar... what is to be done with one's life? I simply don't know...' By the time Wilde was reinterred at Père-Lachaise, a decade later, Lord Alfred had found the answer, having embraced Catholicism with a zealousness that would match Crowley's occult devotion and like The Beast, he had also married. However, Lady Olive Douglas (née Custance), a colonel's daughter, kept the ring on her finger longer than Lady Rose Boleskine (née Kelly.) Having obtained a divorce, Rose departed from Crowley's life in November, 1909, coinciding with the intensification of the relationship between The Beast and the visionary poet Victor Neuburg. A superlative account of their union is given by Jean Overton Fuller in *The Magical Dilemma of Victor Neuburg*. With Aleister Crowley acting as Guru to Neuburg's student/seer, their Magickal workings were potent enough to break the devotee's mental and physical health, ably abetted by beatings with gorse and nettles; 'A homosexual sadist' was how Victor affectionately referred to his esoteric master in his notes. Although Crowley berated Neuburg for his Jewish ancestry, The Beast nonetheless remained in touch with his family, issuing a telegram that read 'Send £500 or you will never see your son again.' Unsurprisingly, this brought about the desired results. There is no doubt that Aleister Crowley was a mystic and magician who sought to rip asunder the confines of life but there was a price to pay, as Jean Overton Fuller attested: 'If ever a man went off his head through the occult sciences, it was Crowley.'

Many years after Neuburg had cut ties with The Beast, cowed by the belief that Aleister Crowley had cursed him, Lord Alfred Douglas paid a visit to Victor's home on the Sussex Downs. The reason for the call is not specified in Overton Fuller's book but he never got over the threshold, Victor's wife, Kathleen, unceremoniously shutting the door in his face. Perhaps she feared it was in some way connected to The Beast's anti-Bosie poems dating back to 1910, when Neuburg had still been in Crowley's thrall. The poems, 'The Child' and 'A Slim Gilt Soul' dedicated to 'Lord A' had appeared in a collection of The Beast's work under the title *The Winged Beetle*. In a handsome 1992 facsimile edition of *The Winged Beetle* (Teitan Press) editor Martin P. Starr makes a curious observation in the introduction, stating that 'A Slim Gilt Soul' ... 'Is alleged to have provoked the highly litigious Douglas to pursue Crowley in court but to no avail.'

Though eminent in his Beastly knowledge, Starr's wording is evasive and misleading. Some clarity is shed upon the matter in *Oscar Wilde and The Black Douglas*. (1949) Written by Bosie's nephew, the book does Lord Alfred few favours save for this one: 'In 1910 that enigmatic and somewhat sinister personage, the late Aleister Crowley, honoured Bosie – whom one gathers he did not like – with a lampoon in the best eighteenth-century manner. For once Bosie did not take action. In this he was well advised. Aleister Crowley was a rich man and an experienced litigant, with a power of invective that left nothing to be desired.' One has the sense that The Beast was chomping at the bit for Bosie to take the bait and 'A Slim Gilt Soul' was the opening salvo – as the first three verses establish.

'Few men are given, 'twixt heaven and hell,
To play one part supremely well.
On all time's tablets there are few
Who make a first-rate show of two,

While those who perfectly play three
We knew not, until you were he.

For what were lovelier on the lawn
Than you, pearl-naked to the dawn,
Wrapped in a scarlet dressing-gown
Not thirty miles from London town,
That "observed of all observers" – save
That Scotland Yard, serene and suave,
When trouble came, went tramping by;
Closed one, and winked the other eye.

How pleasantly you must have smiled:
"I left them, and I left them wild":
Though certainly they had abhorred
The task of locking up a lord.
For a more tragic role you played
Your master neatly you betrayed.
His shame and torture, turned your leer
To a snarl – your drab's smile to a sneer,
Quickened, when afterwards your help
He needed to a currish yelp...'

In *The King of the Shadow Realm*, John Symonds – biographer of The Beast and his literary executor – observed: 'Early in his life, Crowley made the discovery that he could say untruthful and horrid things about people – that they were prostitutes or drug addicts or thieves or cowards or just "unimaginable shits" – and there the slander would remain or quietly evaporate in the air. Who was to deny it? He did not say these things of course to the person herself. Against the defenceless or those whom he knew were not going to get themselves embroiled with so shocking a person as Aleister Crowley, he would sometimes say malicious things in a letter or in print. It was a characteristic he shared with the paranoid Lord Alfred Douglas.' Was it any wonder Bosie was paranoid? Unfortunately, it was a Douglas family trait, the Marquess of Queensberry suffering from delusions that the 'Oscar Wilders' were after him shortly before the end of his life. As well as acting as Crowley's biographer, Symonds also wrote a mischievous book entitled *Conversations with Gerald* (Duckworth

1974). A playful account of Gerald Hamilton's adventures, the book not only explores Hamilton's recollections of lodging with The Beast in Berlin but also covers his friendship with Lord Alfred Douglas. Early on in 'The Conversations' the subject of Lord Alfred Douglas' mental instability is raised, Hamilton remarking 'Bosie Douglas was a perfect client for a first-class psychiatrist, but in those days psychology had hardly been invented, at least in England.' Symonds seeks to elicit further information: 'Apart from his somewhat obvious persecution mania, were there other symptoms that you noticed?' 'Symptoms of what?' 'Of peculiar behaviour.' 'Isn't persecution mania enough?' said Gerald...

Lord Alfred Douglas was not an astute man, and possessed an uncanny knack for acquiring enemies, which grew as the years darkened. George Bernard Shaw noted the split in Bosie's persona, 'There is Douglas the poet and the hereditary Douglas.' Lord Alfred was a creature of extremes, the louche youth transforming into an ardent Roman Catholic which informed an incipient homophobia and with it a sense of moral righteousness that had Crowley rearing up on his hairy haunches. The irony is that The Beast was just as devout albeit to different Gods, whilst in his *Confessions* he refutes the sexual aspect of his relationship with Pollitt, stating 'To him I was a mind – no more.' Though Aleister Crowley speaks of his former Cambridge lover with immense affection the negation of the erotic elements of the relationship is explained by Lawrence Sutin in *Do What Thou Wilt*: 'Crowley was willing to be iconoclastic when it came to Christianity, but he felt compelled to take a virulent stance against the effeminate decadence as perceived by late Victorian society – of homosexuals.' (St. Martin's Press, 2000) The second of The Beast's anti-Bosie pieces, 'The Child,' an acrostic ode written a year before Bosie's full conversion to the Church of Rome, references one of L.A.D's earlier poems 'Rejected.' Composed in 1896, 'Rejected' finds the poet abandoned by Wilde in the guise of Apollo whilst renouncing Christ and is beautifully wrought, concluding; 'And now I am lost in the mist/ Of the things that can never be/ For I will have none of Christ. And Apollo will none of me.' Crowley lacerates the sentiments: 'Cry out on Apollo; he laughs at the whine/Evoke we a soul nor of man nor divine/Deep-throned in a darker, unspeakable shrine.'

To venerate Wilde's final resting place at Père-Lachaise

cemetery, the sculptor Jacob Epstein designed a controversial monument featuring an exotic winged chimera that manifested facets of Wilde's poem 'The Sphinx' ... 'Whose pallid burden, sick with pain, watches the world with wearied eyes/ And weeps for every soul that dies/ and weeps for every soul in vain.' To preserve the statue's modesty and protect the general public, a tarpaulin was erected to obscure the sphinx's sex. This attempt at art censorship was a red rag to The Beast. On November 5th, 1911, Aleister Crowley, having notified the press of his intentions, visited Père-Lachaise and whipped away the offending tarpaulin. Epstein was less than pleased. To maintain the sphinx's privacy, a butterfly was placed over the offending organ, which The Beast swiped. Returning to London, his appearance at the Café Royal, sporting the butterfly, fig-leaf style, brought a rapturous response from on-lookers. The Café Royal, incidentally, had been a favourite rendezvous of Wilde and Douglas but fortune's wheel had long since turned.

In the poem 'Beauty and the Hunter' Bosie had mused 'Where lurks the shining quarry, swift and shy/ Immune, elusive, unsubstantial? In what dim forests of the soul, where call/ No birds and no beasts creep?' But The Beast still had his quarry in his sites, though he would remain dormant until the baleful contents of *De Profundis* was revealed to Lord Alfred during a court case in April, 1913. From beyond the veil, Douglas was convicted of crimes against the soul by the man he had loved, when the unexpurgated prison letter was made public knowledge. For the second time, Bosie's life went up in flames along with many of the more tender notes that Wilde had written to him, which he burned. Crowley energetically reaped a harvest of withered red rose leaves, including a hypothesis of the events that led to Wilde's trial, which he called 'The Danger of Bunburying' in a correspondence with Robert Hamilton Bruce Lockhart, the British vice-consul in Moscow. The subject is incisively covered by Timothy D'Arch Smith in his leaflet *Bunbury* which contains notes on the subtext of Wilde's play *The Importance of Being Earnest*. A play upon a play upon a play... Crowley's account to the vice-consul alleges that Oscar one day took the train to Banbury and on the journey encountered a young man who he arranged to meet in Sunbury and thus 'Bunbury' came to be. The Beast's theory, as explained to Lockhart, continues... 'For our author (Wilde) began a series of frequent and unexplained absences. The talented author of so many sonnets (Bosie) the same who is now the consummation of purity in English morals, found these absences suspicious and jumped as women [sic] will to a correct conclusion although without definite evidence. There was a tremendous row, and in the event he determined to ruin his friend.' As the author of *The Book of Lies*, Crowley once remarked : 'Keep people ignorant of the facts of nature and make them fighting drunk on bogey tales.' Or should that have been Bosie?

Amongst the many mysteries in the life of Lord Alfred Douglas, perhaps the greatest is why no one gently escorted him to a secluded secret location where he could have concentrated on his consummate poetry and prayed in private, gently sequestered from worldly woes. In the aftermath of the *De Profundis* court case his paranoia would have understandably brought him to a nadir but it was also a well-founded sentiment as outside contrivance had played a part in his public humiliation. Unfortunately, with little impulse control, Lord Alfred was an unmitigated public relations disaster, more often than not tumbling into the claws of his enemies of whom none was archer than The Beast. The idiosyncratic decision to make a gruff tabloid hack, Thomas William Hodgson Crosland, his left-hand man when he became the editor of *The Academy* newspaper in 1907, may be attributed to the irresistible pull between the aristocratic and those of a knavish disposition. However, it could also have been a misconception of masculinity, Bosie's father having been a rough-hewn lout that caused Douglas to appoint as his deputy an irascible, unkempt, alcoholic whose tie he used to straighten prior to social occasions. How far from the days of the finely dressed decadents had Douglas wandered? In its initial phase, *The Academy* had a literary bias, but as time passed and the fading scent of sin was supplanted by papal incense, the paper became political and censorious: 'It has become more than ever important that literature should be kept free from viciousness, prurience and improper suggestion' piped the former pin-up boy of the aesthetic movement. Bosie's poetry also altered, the wonder that he had experienced in the era of Wilde succeeded by religious reveries that on occasion verge on idolomania. Even at their strangest, as 'Prayer for Protestant Children' verifies, fearing as it does for the little darlings 'doomed to keep close company with darkness'...

Douglas could still turn a perfect phrase. The quiet beauty of his finest poetry was now hidden behind the besieged fortress of his heart, whilst his mind fought a thousand screaming battles, just as his blood-maddened ancestors had once done. Crosland became Bosie's attack dog and vicious was he. Worn down by court cases and having lost custody of his son, Raymond, to Colonel Custance, his father-in-law, Bosie foolishly let Crosland loose across the pages of an 'autobiographical account' entitled *Oscar Wilde and Myself* (1914) a bitter rebuke to *De Profundis*. The dark ink of hurt was once again made public, with Crosland as uncouth emissary and Wilde ridiculed and denounced. All was manna to Crowley but it was a book solely credited to Crosland, *The First Stone*, that saw The Beast return in fevered pursuit of Lord Alfred Douglas and his sidekick.

Under the auspices of society hostess Elizabeth Gwendolen Otter a.k.a 'E.G.O.,' two editions of a privately issued pamphlet, *The Writing on The Ground*, were produced in 1913. Displaying the quote 'Whosoever is without sin amongst you let him cast the first stone' on the cover, *The Writing on The Ground* ably demonstrates The Beast's aptitude for rip-roaring malevolence. Both versions of the pamphlet are prefaced by a brief introduction that whilst avoiding naming Douglas, cites Crosland and fangs bared, rounds on the 'Master and his Jackal.' 'A Slim Gilt Soul' is represented in the first and subsequent edition but Crowley's critique of 'The City of The Soul,' which he dubbed 'A Galahad in Gomorrah,' only appears in volume 1. Presented in the manner of a spoof, 'A Galahad in Gomorrah' beseeches Lord Alfred Douglas to condemn the works of an anonymous decadent poet, which commences, 'It is very fortunate that even in times when the greatest laxity of morals prevails, in England at least there is always found some austere and noble soul to protest against decadence; to be a witness in the midst of corruption, that there is a standard of pure and lofty thought, a City of the Soul, fortified against all evil, and whose artillery can overwhelm the savage hordes of impurity. We do not think anyone will accuse us of flattery in saying that Lord Alfred Douglas is just such a person, and this is the more striking phenomenon as it so rare to find true moral greatness associated with poetical genius....'

Rarely has anyone pursued his prey with such ardent devotion as Aleister Crowley. With *The Writing on The Ground*, The Beast had hoped to incite Bosie into a court-room punch-up but was to be sorely disappointed. Proceedings got no further than the somewhat disgruntled aristocrat taking a disconsolate mooch around a block of flats in Chelsea. Unsurprisingly, Crowley's version of events differs from those of Lord Alfred. After Bosie failed to react, Aleister Crowley continued to work thematically, penning *The Writing on The Wall*; 'In its (sic) book *Oscar Wilde and Myself* it professes itself very anxious to persecute the author of *The Writing on The Ground*. The initials of the author were given and her address; my name is also given... "A Galahad in Gomorrah" was republished by Wieland & Co, 33 Avenues S.W. in *The Equinox*, Vol 1 No IX. It took no action. Will it return to England to prosecute ME for criminal libel? "Bosie" is a common prostitute, blackmailer, sodomite, and swindler; and my name is Aleister Crowley, and my address 33 Avenue Studios London S.W.' Paranoid though he might have been and with due cause in this particular instance, Douglas, who refers to the pamphlet as 'The Writing On The Floor' makes no mention of seeking legal recourse in *Oscar Wilde and Myself*:

> ... 'Nobody who lived on any of the floors of these flats, from the basement upwards, would own to the slightest connection with it. I mention these facts not because I attach any importance to the pamphlet but because they show to what extraordinary courses my enemies will have resort when their malice gets the better of them...'

Having failed to drag to Bosie into the dock, from 1913 onwards The Beast employed different and more subtle tactics, including the covert use of names in his fictional works as if needing to remind Lord Alfred that he was still on his case. A short story 'The Ideal Idol' (1918) written under the pseudonym of Cyril Custance is particularly creative. Let us not forget that Custance was the maiden name of Bosie's now estranged wife, Olive. Prefaced as 'Two Stories in One, But With Only One Moral', 'The Ideal Idol' relays the quest of a 42 year old bachelor called Reggie who goes to the States in search of a bride. This is precisely what Douglas had done until his prior association with Wilde had caused

A collection of Lord Alfred Douglas' religious medals, which were in his possession at the time of death.' (Thank you to John Stratford, the Estate of Lord Alfred Douglas)

yet another scandal, whereupon he returned to England and married Olive Custance. By calling the main character Reggie, we again return to Bosie, who was parodied by Robert Hichens in the book *The Green Carnation* (1894) as Lord Reggie Hastings. Though Hichen's satire on the vain young aristocrat, Lord Reggie Hastings and his decadent friend, Mr Esme Amarinth, is relatively good hearted, it was withdrawn when the Wilde trial commenced as the comparisons were all too obvious. *The Green Carnation* concludes with Reggie having a marriage proposal declined and much the same happens in 'The Ideal Idol.'

However, Crowley's narrative sees the spurned Reggie receiving a magical stone from a witch that ensures he will indeed find a bride. The lady in question is one Nina Yolande de Montmorency de Carbajal y Calvados. Retiring to the boudoir after the wedding, the bride screams when she sees the bible and transforms into Mephistopheles, who delivers a sermon: 'Young man!' he said to the astounded Reggie, 'learn that humanity implies imperfection; those who are not content with the ordinary limitations of life, demand perfection, are liable to find the ideal idol an illusion created by the Devil. However, you have willed it, so if you would be so kind as to throw that book out of the window, I will turn back into Nina Yolande (and all the rest of it) and we can get to bed... Bosie, the unwilling muse, was once again at the mercy of The Beast.

The case of 'Bosie and The Beast' must surely be the strangest and most protracted unrequited literary stalking, lasting almost forty years and peaking with *Diary of A Drug Fiend*. Published in 1922, The Beast commits to posterity a pen caricature of Lord Alfred Douglas as 'The Earl of Bumble' described as 'The slight figure of a young-old man with a bulbous nose to detract from his otherwise remarkable beauty, spoilt thought it was by years of insane passions.' At the Earl's heels is his 'jackal,' T.W.H. Crosland, depicted as '... a huge, bloated, verminous creature... in shabby black clothes, ill-fitting, unbrushed and stained.' Though designated a walk-on part in the first chapter, the Earl and the Jackal's entrance causes a stir as The Beast continues: 'The café sizzled as the men entered. They were notorious, if nothing else and the leader was the Earl of Bumble. Everyone seemed to scent some mischief in the air. The earl came up to the table next to mine, and stopped deliberately short. A sneer passed across his lips. He pointed to the two men. 'Drunken Bardolph and Ancient Pistol," he said, with his nose twitching with anger. Jack Fordham was not behind with the repartee. "Well roared, Bottom," he replied calmly, as pat as if the whole scene had been rehearsed beforehand. A dangerous look came into the eyes of the insane earl. He took a pace backwards and raised his stick...' Needless to say, the Earl is given a swift thrashing and ends up prostrate on the floor. Perhaps The Beast felt that by continuing to channel pent-up energies they would impact on Bosie, whose star was not the most stable despite his Christ passion. In religion, Douglas searched for the sanctuary that a turbulent life had failed to offer and with A.C working his tricks, Bosie would have needed one. In pairing the 'Earl of Bumble' with his 'creature,' *Drug Fiend* commemorates an alliance that was already over, Douglas having finally written off his tempestuous friendship with Crosland in a poem entitled 'The Unspeakable Englishman':

> 'You were a brute and more than half a knave,
> Your mind was seamed with labyrinthine tracks
> Wherein walked crazy moods bending their backs

Under grim loads. You were an open grave
For gold and love...'

Between the seven years that separated the publication of *Diary of A Drug Fiend* and *Moonchild* which though written in 1917, wasn't issued until 1929, Aleister Crowley took his foot off the accelerator as far as Lord Alfred Douglas was concerned or perhaps his machinations finally manifested when Bosie riven with paranoia published a leaflet accusing Winston Churchill of participating in a Jewish conspiracy. For reviving gibberish that had long been debunked by those of right minds, Douglas ended up being sentenced to six months stir in Wormwood Scrubs. The Beast meanwhile swanned off to Sicily and founded the Abbey of Thelema, where he honed his now famous credos 'Do What Thou Wilt Shalt Be The Whole of The Law. Love Is The Law, Love Under Will.' Lord Alfred Douglas and Aleister Crowley were polar opposites – Bosie a ruined aristocrat from a bygone era struggling with modernity, The Beast a creature of an aeon that had not yet dawned. Both in their own way predicted the future; Douglas as a youth anticipating an impending century of more liberated sexuality while The Beast unapologetically ushered in the Aquarian age. *Moonchild* was to be the penultimate sputtering of the taper in the one-sided feud that never was. In the novel's brief introduction, Aleister Crowley concludes 'Need I add that, as the book itself demonstrates beyond all doubt, all persons and incidents are purely the figment of a disordered imagination!' The majority of the characters that populate *Moonchild* are drawn from old friends and foes. While the main villain of the piece who is based on Macgregor Mathers, the former head of The Golden Dawn, bears no resemblance to Bosie, The Beast kept enmity's flag flying and called him 'Douglas.' This may also be a reference to the journalist James Douglas who slated *Diary of A Drug Fiend*, thus two birds are killed with one stone. But who threw the first?

As the long night drew closer, Lord Alfred Douglas retired to Hove, where he lived in financial penury but not obscurity. Of superfine manners, Bosie still attracted moths to the myth and made his peace with Oscar Wilde. In his autobiography *A Touch of The Memoirs* (1982) actor Donald Sinden fondly evokes his friendship with Bosie. One rarely mixes with 'dead' people for the youthful Sinden had initially assumed Douglas deceased but happily discovered otherwise though their time would be short: 'So began a series of visits' wrote Sinden of Bosie 'during which he would talk of his childhood, his time in Oxford, the actors he had known – not many – his court cases, books and writers, and gradually the subject of Oscar Wilde, whom he always recalled with great affection. Sometimes tears welled in his eyes.' On March 20th, 1945, Sinden recollects the arrival of a telegram; "'Lord Alfred Died Early This Morning.' Not more than ten of us gathered at his graveside in Crawley as we buried Oscar's 'Rose-lipped youth.' To me, a very kind old man."

No one could have written a finer elegy better than Bosie himself:

'... How sweetly, forged in sleep, come dreams that make
Swift wings and ships that sail the estranging sea,
Less roughly than blown rose-leaves in a bowl,
To harboured bliss. But oh! the pain to wake
In empty night seeking what may not be
Till the dead flesh set free the living soul.'

'The Wastes of Time,' Lord Alfred Douglas, 1934

The Beast felt compelled to leave a final mark in his last collection of poetry, *Olla*, published in 1946, shortly before his own passing. Dedicated to the 'Divine Oscar,' the six line poem entitled 'The Spring of Dirce' does not wax lyrically in its allusion to Lord Alfred Douglas:

'The purple pageant of my incommunicable woes
Was painted by the hand of gin-and-water on my nose.
The mellow gold that filters through my rich autumnal style
Is minted in me by a superfluity of bile.
The feet of Christ I worship at appear so thin and pale
Because of all the skilly that I ate in Reading Gaol.'

Aleister Crowley departed from the world on December 1st, 1947, to the blustery serenade of a thunderstorm as the Old Gods beckoned. Multiple accounts of his death from the average to the mythic circulate, as he would have wished. The Beast was far more astute at engineering a public image than Lord Alfred Douglas. Creator of an 'anti-religion,' The Beast's devotees are legion and he enjoys a prolific cultural afterlife buoyed by an unceasing flow of books, films and articles, whilst the majority of his poetry has been reissued. At Crowley's funeral service, Louis Wilkinson read selected extracts from The Beast's best poem 'Hymn To Pan.' Aleister Crowley had specifically requested that his old friend recite the piece for the past is never far from hand and the circle is unbroken. At the age of 16, Wilkinson, who also wrote under the name "Marlow" had begun a correspondence with Oscar Wilde that was to last until the playwright's death in 1900. Bosie is now regarded as Saint Oscar's scarlet shadow, his poetry more often than not forgotten in the dust of lost dreams.

LIONEL JOHNSON: 'MYSTIC AND CAVALIER'

'To die so futile and so young! A minor Hamlet with Ophelia's death! And at that, his mind turned to Shakespeare, and to a famous modern picture, and to the Lady of Shalott. He imagined himself floating down and down to some mystical medieval city, its torchlights flashing across his white face. But for that, he should be dressed differently, in something Florentine perhaps: certainly not in a comfortable smoking-coat by a London tailor. And at that, he was reminded that a last cigarette would not be out of place: he lighted one and presently fell to wondering whether he was mad or no...'

– Lionel Johnson, 'Incurable,' 1896

Island cottage at Wittersham in Kent was to prove an excellent retreat for one recovering from a shattering nervous breakdown. Now in the quietening years, the poet and critic Arthur Symons no longer pursued those entranced instances which had summoned the uncanny verses of *Stella Maris*, his finest work. Despite the devastating mental collapse that had caused him to all but withdraw from literary life in 1908, Symons was happy to recall the turn of the century demi-monde to which he had once belonged. In the manner of his own dear *Stella Maris* ... 'O lost and wrecked, how long ago, out of the drowning past I know...' Arthur would muse upon those poets known as 'The Tragic Generation.'

A frequent visitor to Island Cottage, the Reverend Montague Summers, whose axiom was 'Tell Me Strange Things,' would have been more than fulfilled by Arthur's vignettes of poetic dissolution. However, as a scholar of the arcane, the Reverend was particularly fascinated by the curious fate of Lionel John-

This photograph taken in 1889, commemorates 22 year old Lionel Johnson becoming the president of the New College Essay Society at Oxford University.

son. Though a poet of some repute if not longevity, Johnson's melancholy verses are wreathed by an eerie foreboding. Largely forgotten, like so many of London's wraiths, Lionel Johnson's frail spectre is said to haunt the scene in Lincoln's Inn that was to have hastened his dispatch. Few cases have been stranger, as Montague Summers reveals in *The Galanty Show* (Cecil Woolf. 1980): 'Arthur would tell the extraordinary story of the death of Lionel Johnson, of the mysterious happenings in his chambers a few days before he was killed, and of the visitants who left the marks of strange claw-like feet. Perhaps they were some bad entities allowed to torment him...'

The youngest son of Captain William Victor Johnson and Catherine Delicia Walters, who were High Church Anglicans, Lionel was born in Broadstairs on March 16th, 1867. It was according to his early letters an 'arid home life' presided over by rigid, narrow-minded parents. There is in the myth of Lionel Johnson something of the lonely watcher in the turret that makes him the male equivalent of Tennyson's 'The Lady of Shalott', for he lived as if under a curse and was never quite of this world. However, there are elements of artful cultivation to his very real tragedy.

Lionel Johnson came of age when the art of mourning was at its (widow's) peak, Queen Victoria having ignited an elaborate death cult when Prince Albert died in December 1861. As the bells tolled for Albert, a sepulchral pall fell across England that would last for nearly forty years. Never before had the veil between this world and the next seemed quite so flimsy, suiting Lionel who searched endlessly for mystical revelation. He would spend his life pursuing that which lies beyond. Even as a teenager he had a fateful inkling that 'I shall leave the world, leave the earthly light, and depart with one thought only: the thought of a life wasted.' (*Winchester Letters*, George Allen. 1919)

In spite of Johnson's morbid proclivities, a piercing sense of humour now and again breaks through like sunlight. Descended from a family with a military tradition but never growing over five foot three, Johnson quipped that the only suitable position would have been that of a drummer boy. Needless to say there was a high mortality rate amongst drummer boys on the battlefield. Lionel's schooling commenced at Clifton Downs in Bristol, until at the age of thirteen, when he entered his beloved Winchester, where he earned the nickname 'Little Bloody.' Having found no good cause for such a spikey moniker one can only presume that it relates to bloody-mindedness for Johnson was of a singularly precocious intellect.

There is no substantial biography of Lionel Johnson; his story is fragmentary, recounted in essays and footnotes, where contradiction collides with paradox. His early death at the age of 35, on October 4th, 1902, created a collusion between censorious family members and concerned friends keen to offer Lionel up as one who had always worn a halo; 'An Angel Visitant,' as G. H. Blore, a Winchester contemporary, described him.

A habitual insomniac, Lionel Johnson took to haunting Winchester by night, immersed in a dream of antiquity that was to become a recurring motif of his poetry...'Wanderings by old-world ways/Walks and streets of ancient days/Closes, churches, arches, halls/Vanished men's memorials...' ('Winchester,' 1888)

It was at college that the mystique begins, fellow student Herbert Fisher remembering Little Bloody as: 'A diminutive, ethereal creature, with a pallid beautiful face, an omnivorous reader, quite remote from the ordinary interests of the school and indeed contemptuous of them, but passionately enamoured of the beauties of Winchester. A certain aura surrounded him for he was reputed to be a Buddhist, to have read all the books in the school library, and to drink eau de cologne for his amusement.' Allegedly, it was a doctor who would recommend alcohol for Johnson's perpetual insomnia but he didn't prescribe 80% proof eau de cologne, a sure sign of a dangerous predisposition to drink.

At sixteen, Lionel destroyed many of his early manuscripts – why we do not know – but succeeded in 'mystifying the House completely on the subject of Spirits: I am rather looking forward to the report of what I did not say in *The Wykehamist*: all the same, ghosts do exist, by 18 to 5! Rather a practical triumph for them.' As Johnson's Winchester letters attest, he discounted Buddhism in favour of Catholicism and considered a future as a priest. A month before his 17th birthday, on February 17th, 1884, he dispatched a cryptic missive to a recipient known only as 'B.' The tone befits the overly serious man-child who sought answers where there should have been none: '... I have often gone into churchyards, and even, when possible, vaults and

Bosie at College. As a prefect, it was Lionel's duty to take insubordinates to be birched, as was the case with 'Bad Boy Bosie.' They soon became fast friends.

charnel houses to try and hear the truth from the lips of spirits, to force the paraphernalia of death to unfold their secret. I have tried, oh so earnestly tried, in utter faith to make the dead hear me, feel for me, comfort me. But the dead are deaf, or else too happy to listen. Don't think me mad...'

With some insight and less pomp than the usual Johnson bystanders, Lord Alfred Douglas later proclaimed to his biographer H. Montgomery Hyde, that... 'Lionel was a delightful fellow, though exceedingly eccentric.' Whilst Johnson was attempting to channel auguries from the realm of shades, a very real portent, in the form of the gregarious Lord Alfred, joined the ranks at Winchester. Three years Johnson's junior, Lord Alfred Douglas who went by the pretty soubriquet of 'Bosie' (an abbreviation of his childhood nickname 'Boysie') was to have a profound effect on Little Bloody's life. Clearly Winchester was not all doom and gloom. Lionel had made a start on his creative vocation by winning several literary prizes, acting as editor on the school paper, *The Wykehamist*, and enjoying the perks of being a prefect by accompanying Douglas when he was birched by the headmaster for a misdeed, an event that Little Bloody would never allow Bosie to forget and which caused the older boy much amusement.

In 1884, Lionel's parents decamped to a decaying mansion in North Wales, where they would reside for the next three years. It was to prove an excellent summer haunt for Johnson, providing the long walks and desolate countryside that inspired his love of folklore and gave an epic quality to his isolation. Along with Wales, Lionel would also tap into the romantic myths of Ireland and Cornwall, a ghost calling to ghosts, his poetry noticeably empty of humanity and its follies, for only the lambent dead and the elements would suffice: 'And nature's violent graces waken there/And there goes loveliness about the grave/ And death means dreaming, not life's long despair.' ('Gwynedd', 1888) With youth's gauzy lack of insight but lashings of insouciance, Johnson summarised his thoughts on relationships with pen-pal Edgar Jepson in 1884, explaining: 'Companionship is, I admit, an essential delight; but I am too calm and cold to pine for it as a want: I enjoy it as a situation, a sensation – I am incapable of hysterics and heroics, even spiritually. The rest of alert acquiescence will result in the self-sufficiency which is so admirable.'

This veneer would crack soon enough. Johnson's self-sufficiency found the companionship of alcohol, the pain spilling over in the handful of poems that truly come from the heart, where his agonised voice can be fully heard. The rest of his verses are themes and ghosts, romantic notions and shadow-plays, a sublimation of desire in the reign of Queen Victoria, where despite a thriving underworld and creative culture, to be homosexual meant the harshest legal penalties.

There was a breakable quality about Lionel Johnson, as if he were a beautifully crafted cut glass figurine, but he was not without mischief as a photograph taken at Oxford University, in 1889, demonstrates. The picture commemorates his role as president of the New College essay society. Twenty-two years old and trapped in a child's frame, Lionel challenges the camera directly, resolutely staring it down.

Few have been as aware of their fate as Johnson and he had already accepted its ivory hand in troth, as 'Mystic and Cavalier' written that same year reveals. One of his finest and most prophetic poems, the opening line maps his future with chilling clarity: 'Go from me: I am one of those, who fall.' The mystique that had accrued at Winchester was to follow the young poet to university and was described by his friend Campbell Dodgson, thus: 'It was whispered that he (Johnson) was the catechumen of strange religious rites which he celebrated in his rooms... and that, finding night and perambulation the only sure provocative of thought, he was in the habit of letting himself out of college in the small hours.'

Whilst the other students slept, Johnson like a moon-struck spectre flitted amidst Oxford's gothic splendour penning moody verses: 'Cool pavements, carved with legends of the tomb: Grave haunts, where we might dream, and understand.' ('Oxford' 1890) It was no wonder then that when Oscar Wilde visited Oxford in February 1890, during daylight hours, Lionel was to be found recumbent, snoozing under a mountain of books.

Oscar Wilde had travelled from London to the university to see Walter Pater, the renowned author and Oxford don. On Pater's recommendation, Wilde dropped Johnson a note. Not yet in his play-writing ascendency but enjoying the infamy that the publication of the magazine version of *The Picture of Dorian Gray* had bestowed, Oscar Wilde was already an eminent force.

When he strode into Oxford, an expanded version of *Dorian Gray* which was to be issued in book form was underway. Though a seasoned journalist, poet and author of children's stories, it was *The Picture of Dorian Gray* that would make Oscar Wilde a sensation. As Lionel tumbled out of bed to meet Wilde, the petite poet had the alacrity to remember his cigarettes, which was just as well as Oscar smoked them all. Johnson forgave him, a detail which he shared in a letter to Arthur Galton: 'On Saturday at mid-day, lying half-asleep in bed... I was roused by a pathetic and unexpected note from Oscar: he plaintively besought me to get up and see him. Which I did: and found him delightful. He discoursed with infinite flippancy; of everyone... and consumed all my cigarettes. I am in love with him...'

Oscar Wilde and Lionel Johnson were both passionate about literature but they could not have been more different. Married with two children and embroiled in an affair with Robbie Ross, who would become his literary executor, Wilde was a dandy, gourmand, taste-maker, scene-stealer and an unsurpassable conversationalist. Small surprise then, that Johnson had so easily fallen under the sophisticated older man's spell and continued a friendship with him. Although his room possessed an ever present jug of whisky, fresh flowers and a copy of Baudelaire's *Les Fleurs Du Mal*, which could be construed as markers of decadence, Lionel Johnson was an aesthete rather than a fop, who perceived literature as a 'Thing of beauty, blood and nerves.' (*The Cultured Faun*, 1891) A retiring, austere young man, he ate little, subsisting mainly on tea, cigarettes, alcohol and the company of books. Night had always been his preferred domain and Lionel enjoyed the kind of intense nocturnal debates that made even the moon rub her eyes in exhaustion. Few of his contemporaries had the capacity for Johnson's all-night vigils, save for Lord Alfred Douglas who arrived at Oxford in Lionel's final year. As Douglas explained to H. Montgomery Hyde:

'He (Lionel) had a mania for not going to bed, and if he could get anyone to sit up with him he would discourse in a most brilliant way till five o'clock in the morning. At other times of the day he was rather noticeably silent. He was a great scholar, and undoubtedly a great poet but the austerity and profundity of his best work makes him one who is never likely to appeal to any but a very eclectic audience. It was one of the griefs of his later years that he introduced me to Wilde.'

As lithe and lovely as a Burne-Jones knight, Lord Alfred was the inspiration for Johnson's poem 'A Dream of Youth,' to whom it was dedicated. In his excellent book *Lord Alfred Douglas – A Poet's Life and His Finest Work* (Peter Owen, 2007), author Caspar Wintermans posits that Johnson and Bosie may have been lovers. Although their correspondence has been lost, an obvious fondness existed between the two and the intention of 'A Dream of Youth' is unmistakable: 'With rippling hair; and gleaming eyes, wherein a sea of passion of lies; Hair waving back, and eyes that gleam With deep delight of dream on dream.' And it was in a dream that Lionel would give Bosie a copy of *The Picture of Dorian Gray*. This novel was the greatest example of English literary decadence, and was to have a profound effect on the young aristocrat. Lionel was equally enamoured of Wilde's creation, dropping the author a verse in Latin, which would remain untranslated and unpublished until after his death:

'Blessed be you, Oscar! Who deem me worthy of this book For friendship's sake: Modulating in the Roman mode Praise to the Dorian owed, I give you thanks. / Here the lovely rose Flourishes amid the roses When suddenly comes death: Behold the Man! Behold the God! O that his mode of pitying Genius were but mine! / Avidly he loves strange loves, Savage with beauty Plucks strange flowers: The more his soul is darkened, His face displays its brightness more.'

Wilde's occult literary masterpiece is an epic of seduction and corruption; a cautionary tale of a beautiful yet malleable young aristocrat who is played like a harp by a Mephistophelean older man, Lord Henry Wotton, who leads Dorian into temptation. In *The Picture of Dorian Gray*, the author alludes to a mysterious book, believed to be based on Huysman's *A rebours*:

'It was a poisonous book. The heavy odour of incense seemed to cling about its pages and to trouble the brain.

The mere cadence of the sentences, the subtle monotony of their music, so full as it was of complex refrains and movements elaborately repeated, produced in the mind of the lad, as he passed from chapter to chapter, a form of reverie, a malady of dreaming, that made him unconscious of the falling day and creeping shadows.'

But it was Wilde's creation that was to cast a greater and more grievous enchantment, for never has such a potent form of psychic vampirism been unleashed from the page and with such unfortunate results. The artist becomes conjuror, summoning powerful entities over which they have no control.

Johnson, like Wilde, would create his own 'Dark Angel,' whose distant presence is palpable in a poem entitled 'Magic' in 1887. 'Mine is the sultry sunset, when the skies Tremble with strange, intolerable thunder: And at the dead of an hushed night, these eyes Draw down the soaring oracles winged with wonder. From the four winds they come to me, The Angels of Eternity.'

Leaving Lord Alfred Douglas in Oxford, where he was reported to have read *The Picture of Dorian Gray* at least 14 times (a conservative estimate), Lionel Johnson moved to London. He took rooms above the offices of the Century Guild of Artists, known as 'The Fitzroy Settlement.' Located at 120 Fitzroy Street at the heart of the city, 'the settlement' was the home of *The Century Guild Hobby Horse*, a magazine dedicated to the aesthetic movement. It also housed not only studios but writers and artists such as the Guild's founding father Arthur Mackmurdo and Johnson's university pal, Arthur Galton, who was destined for the priesthood. In spite of Johnson's early ambitions to become a priest, he didn't follow in Galton's footsteps, pursuing instead the poet's calling after William Butler Yeats asked him to join the Rhymers Club.

Few vocations are as ideally suited to the disordering of the senses as poetry and for Johnson, membership of the Rhymers Club would permanently uncork the bottle. Their meetings were known for liquid libations. Comprising of twelve poets, including Yeats, Arthur Symons, Ernest Dowson, Victor Plarr, Ernest Rhys and Richard Le Gallienne, the Rhymers regularly gathered at the Cheshire Cheese Pub in Fleet Street, to hone their craft.

Having known one another at Oxford, where it was rumoured that they experimented with drugs – most probably hashish – Lionel Johnson and Ernest Dowson palled up once again, bound by poetry and a fatal taste for alcohol.

Although The Rhymers were not adherents of the flamboyant neurosis associated with decadent literature, and had a suing system for anyone who dropped a lily into a sonnet, Lionel and Ernest were both partial to absinthe. Not only did absinthe have a dangerously high alcohol content but the addition of wormwood gave 'The Green Fairy' a psychotropic effect. Cheaper than wine, it was a perfect yet lethal intoxicant for the artistic and the down at heel. In spite of his asceticism, there is an exaggerated morbidity about Johnson that makes him a decadent by default. Absinthe with its rituals and poisonous mystique would have appealed to Lionel's poetic nature but he was not without irony: 'Night fell fast and very gloomy, with scarce a star. Leaning upon the gate, he tried to remember the names of modern poets who have killed themselves: Chatterton, Gerard De Nerval. They at least could write poetry, and their failure was not in art. Yet he could live his poetry, as Milton and Carlyle, he thought had recommended: live it by dying...' (L.J., *Incurable*, 1896)

One night after the pubs shut and Dowson had swanned off to Soho, Lionel asked Richard Le Gallienne back to his rooms, commenting as he climbed the stairs: 'I hope you drink absinthe, for I have nothing else to offer to you.' In his memoirs of the 1890's, Le Gallienne, a novice to absinthe, describes his initiation with Johnson; 'I had just heard of it (absinthe) as a drink mysteriously sophisticated and even Satanic... it was spoken with a self-conscious sense of one's being desperately wicked, suggesting diabolism and nameless iniquity. So it was with a pleasant shudder that I watched it cloud our glasses as I drank it for the first time, there alone with Lionel Johnson, in the small hours, in a room paradoxically monkish in its scholarly austerity.'

Whilst Johnson's output was considerable, for by now he was contributing to numerous magazines and periodicals, including *The Hobby Horse*, which published 'A Dream of Youth', his drinking was already causing concern. The dandified Le Gallienne feared that absinthe was 'too fierce a potion' for the delicate Lionel but it also held a terrible fascination as he surmised:

'because, particularly in the form of his (L.J's) favourite absinthe, it had for a time so quickening and clarifying an effect on the intellectual and imaginative faculties.' However the consequences were debilitating. After another session with Dowson at 'The Fitzroy Settlement,' Johnson tumbled down the stairs, a lit candle in his hand as he showed Ernest to the door. The unfortunate incident did not pass unnoticed by the Guild's founding father, Arthur Mackmurdo. In 'London Town' which Lionel dedicated to Mackmurdo, the unsteady poet wonders... 'Is mine too tragical a strain, Chaunting a burden full of pain, And labour, that seems all in vain? I sing but truth...'

A modest private income enabled Lionel Johnson to all but disengage from the time-keeping that governs the working day; inevitably, this disassociation rendered him increasingly inaccessible: '... Yeats called on Johnson one afternoon at five and found the servant saying "He is always up for dinner at seven."' On another occasion, fellow poet Ernest Rhys... 'Once went on a Rhymers night to collect Johnson at 9pm and the servant boy said "I don't think he's up yet, sir." Rhys went to find him in his darkened room and Johnson said in a small voice he was "too busy to go to the club." (*Madder Music, Stronger Wine*, Jad Adams, Taurus Parke) Lionel Johnson had always possessed the qualities of a shut-in, one who lives as if besieged, but from what? His quiet voice suggests exhaustion, the décor in his room that of an ascetic sanctuary. Aside from one of Simeon Solomon's dreamy paintings, Johnson's taste was notably churchy and included a gothic monstrance such as those used to contain consecrated wafers, a large silver crucifix and a picture of Cardinal Newman; bulwarks of protection rather than ornamentation. And it is only in day-light, surrounded by his holy relics that he attempts to rest: 'Dear, are there dreams among the dead: Or is it all a perfect slumber? But I must dream and dream to madness.' ('The Beyond,' 1889)

Unperturbed by Lionel's erratic hours and impressed by his lyricism, W.B. Yeats would do much for him as both a friend and influence. Drawn by the romanticism of Yeats's 'Celtic Twilight', Johnson embraced mystical Ireland as both a creative inspiration and a spiritual home. On at least one occasion the two men travelled to Ireland to deliver a lecture on poetry which was witnessed by Yeats's sister, Elizabeth, who wrote of Lionel

Johnson: 'I think no man ever saw him angry or petulant, or till his infirmity had grown on him, shaken from his self-possession and it often seemed as if he played at life, as if it were an elaborate ritual that would soon be over. I am certain he had provision of his end, and that he was himself that mystic and cavalier who sang: "Go from me, I am one of those, who fall...."'

Protective though he was of Johnson, whose fragility he recognised, W.B. Yeats told his friend, the folklorist Augusta Gregory, that 'Johnson is quite safe at dinner. He does his drinking mostly in his own rooms.' (*W.B. Yeats: A Life*. RF Foster, Oxford University Press) Johnson, though on a precarious path, was at least maintaining a life but the year of 1891 was to be a significant one from which the arc of his descent can be measured. A letter dated February 5th, 1891, to Campbell Dodgson, shows the poet in ill-health and low spirits: 'I have been in the depths of misery all through this weary autumn and insufferable winter. To begin with the venomous fogs have nearly blinded me, and oculists have tortured me to death. I may have to go to a man at Lausanne in the spring.' More encouragingly, Lionel's brother sent him 2,000 cigarettes from Cairo, too many for even Oscar Wilde to have smoked his way through. Though not a member of the Rhymers Club, their regular venue, The Cheshire Cheese, being a little too rustic and bohemian, Oscar Wilde attended at least two of their meetings when they were held in more pleasing settings, which Lionel mentions to Campbell in the same letter: 'We entertained the other night eighteen minor poets of our acquaintance: from Oscar Wilde to Walter Crane, with Arthur Symons and Willie Yeats between. They all inflicted their poems on each other...'

In an unusually upbeat mood, Lionel hailed the summer as a poet must, with some new verses: 'Winter is gone! Soon comes July/ With wafts from hayfields by and by: While in the dingiest courts you spy Flowers fair to see...' ('London Town' 1891) Oxford University had broken up for the summer holidays and Lord Alfred Douglas, a flower fair to see, was staying in town with his mother in elegant Cadogan Place. As he had promised, Johnson took a hansom cab to pick Bosie up and off they went to visit Oscar Wilde at his house in Tite Street, Chelsea.

The meeting was to have far reaching consequences and has left Johnson vulnerable to certain Wilde scholars, such as

Thomas Wright who mars his otherwise valuable *Oscar's Books* (Vintage) by deriding him as a 'Prematurely aged... Pierrot like homunculus', which differs greatly from a first-hand description of Lionel at the time by W.B. Yeats, in which he is depicted as 'Determined and erect... almost a dwarf but beautifully made, his features cut in ivory.' (*Aesthetes and Decadents of the 1890's*, Academy Chicago)

By contrast with Wright's scathing description of Lionel, Lord Alfred fortunately passes muster as an 'Adonis,' before being summed up with Wilde's oft used adage about 'life imitating art' in the Douglas/Dorian trope. Oscar, at almost thirty-seven, had been instantly smitten by the nineteen year old aristocrat. Johnson's innocent gesture of introducing Lord Alfred to Wilde was to prove cataclysmic for all three of them. As author Rupert Crooke Cooke explains;

> 'He (L.J.) was not a silly, well-meaning little man, but a creature of vision and intuition who believed that these two were made for one another. In his later years, before and after the Wilde catastrophe, it was a grief to him that he brought them together for he never lost his devotion to Bosie and believed that Wilde was wrecking his friend's life.' (*Bosie*, pub W.H Allen)

That same decisive summer, in which Wilde commenced his wooing of Lord Alfred Douglas, saw Johnson being received into the Roman Catholic faith by Fr. William Lockhurt, an associate of Cardinal Newman. Subsequently, Lionel attempted to convert Ernest Dowson, who capitulated but with less vigour. Unfortunately, they drank more than the blood of Christ. In a 1936 radio broadcast, W.B. Yeats told the BBC, 'Some friends of mine saw them one moonlit night returning from The Crown public house which had just closed, their zigzagging feet requiring the whole width of Oxford Street, Lionel Johnson talking. My friend stood still eaves-dropping, Lionel Johnson was expounding a Father of the Church. Their piety, in Dowson, a penitential sadness, in Lionel Johnson more often a notable ecstasy, was as I think, illuminated and intensified by their contrasting puppet shows, those elegant, tragic penitents.'

As he had commenced the year with a letter to Campbell

Dodgson, so Lionel Johnson concluded it, sombrely noting:

> 'I am writing in my arm chair by the fire: I have an arm
> chair now, and I live in it: so my delicate scripture will
> probably be more than commonly dark. Here I have
> been enlightening the world through the columns of
> some half dozen papers since October: very busy and
> rather ill: my doctor says grim things about spinal pa-
> ralysis which annoy/worry me. I lately refused an invi-
> tation to go to Yokohama for a year, to recover health
> under cherry trees upon the lower slopes of Fusijama.
> Lucky, I didn't go: for Fusijama has been vomiting lava
> by the square mile...'

In spite of his faltering health, Lionel was active, as he informs
Dodgson, lecturing at several Catholic societies and holding
forth to a lively audience on the Gordon riots, whilst continuing his association with the Rhymer's Club as well as writing a
book on Thomas Hardy. There is an element of Johnson trying
to cram everything in, whilst his faculties still allow. What might
the onset of 'Spinal Paralysis' have meant to a young man... a
lack of balance, difficulty in walking, a tendency to fall. If Lionel's deportment as Yeats noted was 'Determined and erect'
was it through effort? Of Johnson the sources tend to presume
drunkenness, the zigzagging gait of the bar-hopper, a tipsy tumble down the stairs – for he was an alcoholic – but what if his
dipsomania was the symptom not the cause? Again we return to
Mystic and Cavalier, written over two years earlier, for none is
more relevant to his mystery as each descending verse carries
him further away: 'The clouds are breaking from the crystal ball,
Breaking and clearing; and I look to fall.'

Having returned to Oxford, Bosie was doing rather better
as the editor of *The Spirit Lamp*, a student paper, than at his
studies. The inaugural issue was launched on May 6th, 1892 and
was published on a weekly basis for a little over a year, boasting
an impressive roll-call of contributors including Oscar Wilde,
Arthur Symons, Lord Alfred Douglas and Lionel Johnson. One
early edition contains a 'spoof' telegram from a certain 'Lady
D'Escarville' to her unnamed son that warns: 'Your connection with the new paper, *The Spirit Lamp*, pleases me, though I

should not get too literary, as people will always think you are a radical or a bohemian or something dreadful of that sort.'

Johnson submitted one poem 'A Friend,' a literary criticism entitled 'The Purgatory' and a gently humorous piece, 'Sad True Incident In the Life Of A Critic.' Though well-written, none are particularly striking save for a depiction of the poet contained in 'Sad True Incident' which sees him enjoying a splendidly book-ish isolation: 'My fire, my candles, my curtains, the gleaming backs of my books. Warmed my heart to all the world... I was luxurious in my sympathy to the entire universe: for not a man had come near me the whole long day.' His reveries are broken by a caller. Given the line-up of contributors to *The Spirit Lamp*, one assumes creative unity, but seemingly out of nowhere, like the volcano in Fusijama that he had managed to avoid, Lionel suddenly erupted and sent spinning into the ether a most fear-some missive: 'The Destroyer of a Soul.' Lionel Johnson, usually the most demure of young men, even when drunk, was rendered apoplectic with rage and loss.

The Destroyer of a Soul

'I hate you with a necessary hate.
First, I sought patience: passionate was she:
My patience turned in very scorn of me,
That I should dare forgive a sin so great,
As this, through which I sit disconsolate;
Mourning for that live soul, I used to see;
Soul of a saint, whose friend I used to be:
Till you came by! A cold, corrupting fate.

Why come you now? You, whom I cannot cease
With pure and perfect hate to hate? Go, ring
The death-bell with a deep, triumphant toll!
Say you, my friend sits by me still? Ah peace!
Call you this thing my friend? This nameless thing?
This living body, hiding its dead soul?'

There has been conjecture about the poem's recipient and the subject but the sonnet was addressed to Oscar Wilde and the soul is that of Lord Alfred Douglas. (*Lord Alfred Douglas*, H.

Montgomery Hyde, Methuen) Finally, the poet had realised that he had been supplanted by Wilde in Bosie's affections.

Although Lionel would continue to contribute alongside Oscar to several publications including *The Chameleon*, he severed relations with Wilde, whilst remaining loyal to Lord Alfred. One of Lionel Johnson's favourite adages, according to W.B. Yeats, was 'Life is ritual.' There is in Johnson's story a perpetual need to maintain balance and makes all the more sense why upon learning that Douglas was faltering in his studies, Lionel suggested additional tutoring and put forward his friend Campbell Dodgson. The decision was made after Johnson and Bosie spent February 1893, vacationing at the Salisbury home of Lord Alfred's mother, Lady Queensberry. But was Johnson's proposition entirely altruistic? By deploying Dodgson with whom he corresponded, the little poet was kept well-informed.

The tutoring arrangement quickly fell apart after Campbell and Douglas went to stay at Oscar's seaside retreat at Babbacombe Cliff. The study time-table devised by Wilde and observed by Dodgson was more than convivial but not particularly scholarly: 'Breaks for sherry, lunch, "compulsory hide and seek," brandy and sodas and dinner with "compulsory champagne."' As Douglas Murray notes in *Bosie* (Hyperion): 'Wilde himself told Dodgson that "I have succeeded in combining the advantages of a public school with those of a private lunatic asylum, which was as you know, my aim."' One can imagine Johnson tutting disapprovingly as he received Campbell's reports for he knew more than anyone that the years were not for frittering and his would be few. 1893-1894 was the last period in which Lionel Johnson was able to properly engage on a social level. But he was not yet spent creatively, even if the candle was sputtering. When not immured in shadows, Johnson was capable of being sparklingly funny as 'On The Appreciation of Trifles,' which was published in *The Chameleon* in December, 1894, demonstrates. For a rare moment, he discards the shroud for a glittering repartee that warns against thrift: 'Economy is a grievous evil... There are many whose lives are a constant protest against this vice and the evil practices it entails...' for it was in the small, fine things that Lionel took pleasure: soap, scent and liveried servants.

It wasn't just life that Lionel Johnson perceived as ritual, but death as well and by the age of twenty-seven, he was in dress-rehearsal. He had never known what it meant to be in robust health: 'The end is set: Though the end be not yet,' he had written in 'Mystic and Cavalier.' Shored up against the night with his monstrance and crucifixes, he informed W.B. Yeats that anyone who didn't believe in eternal damnation was 'vulgar.' Hell, we can only assume from Johnson's point of view must have been an extraordinarily bad-manned place; a little like London today. Though Lionel Johnson was ardent in his conversion, he was also an aesthete and no one does death quite like the Catholic Church: 'Vanquished in life, his death by beauty made amends.' (L.J., 'By the Statue of King Charles at Charing Cross')

Although *The Art of Thomas Hardy* had been well received, it was the work of an obsessive, the words rigidly bound together as if Lionel were scared that they, much like himself, would fall apart. He must now manage what was increasingly beyond him; control a body that won't do as it's told, quench a thirst that is never slaked, and extinguish those passions that still burn. In a short space of time – he had so little left now – Lionel wrote a trilogy of infernal hymns: 'Vinum Daemonum,' 'Satanas' and 'The Dark Angel,' products of the madness that insists upon his staying up all night long, fasting in preparation for communion the next morning, laying more torment on his frail body. He must not oversleep! He must not drink! The bottle glistens on the mantelpiece, beautiful by candlelight, its name 'Vinum Daemonum'...: 'But only watch the wild-wine glow, But only taste its fragrance: then, Drink the wild drink I bring and so Reign among men. Only one sting, and then but joy: One pang of fire and thou art free. Then what thou wilt, thou can't destroy: Save only me...'

In April, 1894, Lionel Johnson attended a launch party at the Hotel D'Italie on Old Compton Street for *The Yellow Book*, a subversive new arts magazine featuring Aubrey Beardsley's illustrations. Also present were Ernest Dowson and W.B. Yeats, whilst Lionel had invited his cousin, Olivia Shakespear, the only family member in whom he could confide. What cruel irony as once again, Lionel so lonesome he could die, reprised his role of match-maker, introducing his dear cousin to his dear friend, Yeats. Although married, albeit unhappily, Olivia subsequently embarked on a long term relationship with W.B. Yeats.

One of the sweetest of Johnson's poems, 'Lines To A Lady

Upon Her Third Birthday,' is a dedication to Olivia's daughter, Dorothy, yet even the kindly sign off 'And I, Despite all dark fates, Dorothy, Will prove me thine affectionate Cousin, and loyal laureate,' is heavy with sad portents. It is through Yeats's compassionate eyes that we learn most of Lionel Johnson, who at the point of *The Yellow Book* launch was immersed in his satanic trinity. Writing of Johnson in *Autobiographies*, Yeats pondered: 'Did the austerity, the melancholy of his thoughts, that spiritual ecstasy which he touched at times, heighten as complementary colours heighten one another, not only the Vision of Evil, but it's fascination?' Viewed now, 'Satanas' which was originally composed in Medieval Latin verges on the unhinged as Lionel lays his charges at Lucifer: 'The Prince of the world rejoices, Beholding the soul confounded; He delights to watch, The death-throes of the heart. The gasping heart, at point of death, Seeks vain things, vainly searching; The flames clinging to the soul torture, The most disconsolate heart. The rector of gloom rejoices, To sacrifice the bitter heart....' The entire piece is considerably longer and harrowing in the extreme, making it impossible to align the author with the same Lionel Johnson who was capable of writing something as playful as 'On the Appreciation of Trifles.'

The two poets from the Rhymers Club that W.B. Yeats would eulogise as the star-crossed essence of 'The Tragic Generation' were Lionel Johnson and Ernest Dowson. Desperate though drink might have made them, Yeats perceived something poetic in their abandonment, the drowning on dry land that gives them a kinship to Arthur Symons's unearthly *Stella Maris*. Drawing from Yeats's *Autobiographies*, Jad Adams paints a grimly humorous picture in *Madder Music, Stronger Wine* where 'Johnson fancied he was a good influence on Dowson, which (Arthur) Symons joked was limited to those times when Dowson had heard enough about the Fathers of the Church and declared his intention to go and look for a "ten-penny whore", and Johnson would encourage him to stay to have another drink instead....' Both were in their cups, but it was Dowson who would dedicate a poem entitled 'Extreme Unction' to Lionel Johnson.

The sacrament of the last rites, 'Extreme Unction,' is performed by a priest when death is imminent. Lionel personified his torment in his best known poem 'The Dark Angel'; the third and final satanic presage from his infernal trinity. Originally published in June 1894, in the second Rhymer's club anthology, 'The Dark Angel' is Lionel Johnson's 'Dorian Gray,' an expression of the shadow-side, compromising of fourteen verses, of which the first four set the searing tone:

'Dark Angel, with thine aching lust
To rid the world of penitence:
Malicious Angel, who still dost
My soul such subtle violence!

Because of thee, no thought, no thing,
Abides for me undescecrate:
Dark Angel, ever on the wing,
Who never reachest me too late!

When music sounds, then changest thou
It's silvery to a sultry fire:
Nor will thine envious heart allow
Delight untortured by desire

Because of thee, the land of dreams
Becomes a gathering place of fears:
Until tormented slumber seems
One vehemence of useless tears...'

With a dreadful but not unexpected synchronicity, Johnson's decline hastened in 1895, the year of Wilde's arrest, trial and imprisonment. Oscar Wilde was left broken, ruined, and the reputation of Lord Alfred Douglas never to recover.

Unlike many of Bosie's friends who snubbed him after the trial, Johnson remained devoted. Advised to leave England, Lord Alfred went into exile in Europe, where he crossed from France to Italy in disconsolate mood. Johnson did what he could; as well as spending time with Lord Alfred, he also sent a letter imploring a mutual friend, More Adey, to encourage others to visit the young aristocrat, in which he stressed: 'It is very important for Bosie's health and peace of mind, that he should be alone as little as possible', and concluded, 'Most of his Oxford friends seem unable or unwilling for various reasons, to accompany him.'

In his introduction to Lionel Johnson's *Collected Poems* (1953) editor Iain Fletcher writes of Johnson's 'double-life,' leaving one to surmise that aside from Lord Alfred Douglas and Olivia Shakespear, the poet allowed only glimpses of his true self to be seen. How could he have felt safe after the dreadful homophobia that Wilde's trial had made all too apparent? As fellow Rhymer, Victor Plarr observed: 'It is impossible to quote what Lionel Johnson said, for here we should be treading on the ground which is forbidden.'

The moment the guilty verdict came in on Wilde and he was charged with 'Gross Indecency,' art in England changed. Decadent subjects were now viewed as suspect along with anything remotely delicate and a thousand lilies withered and died. The dedication to Lord Alfred on 'A Dream of Youth' silently vanished from all subsequent reprints of Johnson's poems, as did the one to Wilde in 'The Destroyer of a Soul.'

Literature could be censored, but what Lionel Johnson could not disguise was the extent of his drinking. Yeats on several occasions beseeched him to get help, even going so far as suggesting an institution. In *The Trembling Veil,* W.B. Yeats describes one such devastating scene; 'One day when I had been very urgent, he (L.J.) spoke of "a craving that made every atom of his body cry out," and said the moment after, "I do not want to be cured," and a moment after that, "In ten years I shall be penniless and shabby, and borrow half crowns from friends."'

The precariousness of Johnson's situation was magnified when Arthur Mackmurdo dispatched a note in which he asked the poet to leave 'The Fitzroy Settlement' because of his drinking. This was hugely perturbing to Johnson, for he had lived contentedly if not soberly on the premises for five years and was, so he thought, amongst friends. Attempting to dissuade Mackmurdo, the poet wrote him an extremely poignant letter that gives a terrible clarity to Johnson's helplessness: 'I am exceedingly distressed by your letter, though I fully recognise your just cause of complaint. But may I ask for a further trial, upon the condition that I take the pledge at once – which I should have done long ago – that upon giving the least disturbance I go. Also, I promise to have no drink in my rooms but for friends. As long as it depends on my own will, I am quite hopeless: but the pledge is different. I once took it temporarily, for a month and kept it rigidly: and should have taken it for good and all, but for falling ill. If you consent to this, it will be the greatest of many kindnesses...' But Johnson didn't take 'The Pledge,' and Arthur Mackmurdo didn't budge.

The enforced move from 'The Fitzroy Settlement' in September 1895 further destabilised Lionel Johnson. He relocated to comfortable chambers at 7 Gray's Inn Square, which the poet described as 'cloistered, academic and leisurely', but never managed to make another home for himself. Since school, he had boarded in an atmosphere of male camaraderie but his future was that of an unfit tenant, drifting from one set of rooms to the next never quite fitting in; the mournful pale young man upstairs who, despite his shaking hands, has the most perfect manners.

Save for a few remaining creative associates, Johnson gradually detached himself from London's literary life and quarrelled with Ernest Dowson. Sober, Dowson was a gentle man but when drunk he was known to have a fearsome temper, though he would remember little the next day. Who knows what Lionel Johnson recalled as each morning dawned with only his faith to cling to? 'My hatred of myself is pain Beyond My tolerable share...' (L.J., 'To Passions')

At Gray's Inn, Johnson locked the door upon himself as Iain Fletcher explains in the preface to the *Collected Poems* (1953): 'Imperceptibly, he began now to withdraw himself. His friends began to see less of him. Yeats tells us that when he called the milk would be sour at the door and, on the occasions when they did meet, Johnson showed little vitality until the first drink of the evening had been tremulously conveyed to his mouth.'

W.B. Yeats, having felt that he had done everything possible to encourage Lionel to get help, left him to his drink, never to return. However, Yeats subsequently incorporated him into his literary mythology, creating from Johnson's persona a character called Owen Aherne, who author R.F Foster describes as 'a seeker for supernatural wisdom.'

Tragically, Lionel was now in the terminal stages of alcoholism, his small frame unable to withstand the strain his drinking placed upon it. The picture of unmitigated misery, with its sepia tint of whisky and ruby red splashes of port, which Iain Fletcher paints of Johnson staggering between Henekey's and Mooney's in nearby Holborn, could not be more distressing. Yet it was at this precise point that the poet wrote the brilliantly witty essay, 'Incurable.' Published in *The Pageant* in 1896, it is one of the finest examples of gallows humour, elegant and self-knowing, as it parodies both Ernest Dowson, Arthur Symons and himself. Relayed first hand, 'Incurable' is the story of an unnamed suicidal poet on what he hopes will be the final night of his life; 'I am just thirty and quite useless....' Having decided upon drowning as his preferred method of self-immolation, the poet envisions an imaginary friend, a violinist who plays Rameau's 'The Dance of Death.' The poet chastises himself for choosing such an obvious tune...

> 'At the same time, there was something strange and rare in drowning yourself by night to the dance-music of your unconscious friend. The bitter smell of aster and chrysanthemum was heavy in the air; "Balms and rich spices for the sad year's death," as he had once written and he fancied, though he could not be sure that he caught a bat's thin cry.... As "The Dance of Death" whirls on, the poet reads the sonnet he has just written; "Ah, day by swift malignant day, Life vanishes in vanity: Whilst I, life's phantom, play The music of my misery. Draw near, ah dear delaying Death!"'

The violinist materialises and realising the desperate plight of the chain smoking versifier invites him to his imaginary cottage where they can invent a new profession for him.

> 'The unhappy poet brooded upon his futility to write something like the "Ode to Duty" or the "Scholar Gipsy": dust and ashes! Dust and ashes! Suddenly the horror of a long life spent in following the will-o-the wisp or in questing for Sangrails and Eldorados fell upon him: he refused to become an elderly mooncalf. The river haunted him with its facilities for death, and he regretted that there were no water lilies in it...'

Pondering the starless sky, the unfathomable darkness, the poet smokes a second final cigarette as he wanders by the river's edge, his gloomy cogitations suddenly broken when he accidentally falls in the water. In an ungainly pickle, he manages to scramble to the other side of the shore. Much to the poet's acute embarrassment, his imaginary friend, furious for having been given the role of 'Charon' has to row out to rescue him. In spite of the poet being soaked through, 'Incurable' ends happily:

> 'His teeth chattered, and he shook, and he still mumbled bits of verse. Said the musician, as they entered the little cottage: "The first thing for you to do is take off those things and have hot drinks in bed, like Mr. Pickwick." Said the doomed man, quaking like an aspen: "Yes, but I must write out a sonnet first, before I forget it." He did.'

Concurrently to 'Incurable' and underlining the diffuse nature of Lionel Johnson, he also submitted three bone dry poems on religious heretics to *The Savoy*. Edited by Arthur Symons, *The Savoy* was heartily lampooned in *Punch* who referred to it as 'The Savaloy.' The 1890's have been described as a period of transition as a more decorous, courtly age bowed out to a boisterous new century; a curious moment when horse drawn carriages and motor cars could both be seen on the streets of London. As fine as filigree, Lionel Johnson and Ernest Dowson could not have been anything other than Victorians, their misty verses and melancholy countenance rendering them as obsolete as hansom cabs would soon become. They were not meant to last. As Lionel's friend, Edgar Jepson, commented; 'the truth is the 'Nineties came to an end because the poets and artists were tired. In '97, Dowson and Beardsley were tired and so was Lionel Johnson. They had done their best work.'

In May 1898, and despite recurring bouts of influenza, Lionel Johnson visited Dublin for the last time delivering a lecture at the National Literary Society and accepting an invitation to the home of author and Royal Chaplain, Stopford Brooke, who observed: 'Lionel Johnson and Miss O'Brien dined with us. Miss O'Brien is gay and fresh. L. Johnson is mournful and decaying. Both are young, but Johnson is very old... a small dark withered man.'

It was under these sorrowful conditions that the poet moved into a set of chambers on the third floor of 8 New Square, Lincoln's Inn. Traditionally, the rooms in the early Georgian property were used as offices by lawyers during working hours. Aside from a care-taker, who shuffled down to his basement lair once night fell and stayed there, Johnson would have been the sole occupant of the upper most part of the building; his rooms annexed from the rest of the house by a narrow staircase and a sturdy outer door with a heavy latch. The agent had been keen to let the property at an unusually low rent which suited Lionel, who by now was consuming two pints of whisky every twenty four hours. In what fever-dream did Lionel Johnson accept the tenancy? The poet could barely distinguish day from night so tenuous was his febrile grasp on reality. Whilst some might have baulked at such a lonesome dwelling or taken heed of the agent's casual comment about it being the kind of place that appealed to short staying residents, it suited Lionel's needs for he kept much to himself.

On those rare occasions when he did venture out, the troubled poet's appearance was cause for grave concern. As his philosopher friend George Santayana, to whom Lionel had dedicated 'Satanas', noted when they met at a gathering at the Earl of Russell's home in Temple Gardens: 'It was a tragic spectacle. He still looked very young... but pale, haggard and trembling. He stood by the fireplace, with a tall glass of whisky and soda at his elbow, and talked wildly of persecution. The police he said where after him everywhere. Detectives who pretended to be his friends of his friend, Murphy or of his friend MacLaughlin, had to be defied. Without a signed letter of introduction he could trust nobody... as he spoke he quivered with excitement, hatred and imagined terrors. He seemed to be living in a dream...'

In the spirit realm time is but a blink of a sightless eye. How the shadows must have teemed with strange malignancy to one as sensitive as Lionel Johnson. Adjacent to Lionel's latest abode was the picaresque Lincoln's Inn Fields, one of London's largest squares and pretty enough when the sun shone. The grass had long since grown over the site where crowds had gathered to witness the execution of Lord Anthony Babbington in 1586. He was accused of plotting to murder Elizabeth I and was sentenced to be hung, drawn and quartered. Taken half-alive from the gallows and still conscious when evisceration began, Lord Anthony is said to return to the scene of his horrendous demise.

One can only hope that Lord William Russell, who was behead-
ed on the same spot in 1683 for devising an assassination attempt on Charles II, has been granted the peace that was denied
to Babbington.

Lincoln's Inn, in common with other singularly haunted
spots, gave the impression of being a province of its own, separate from the life-blood of ordinary London, especially when
the shadows lengthened. Once the lawyers and their clerks hurried home to the suburbs, an imperceptible mist clung about
the place. The care-taker shut out the night at 8 New Square,
when he bolted the front door at the end of each working day,
but the terror came from within or more precisely the upper
reaches of the property. An uncanny miasma enveloped the
chambers where Lionel Johnson now resided, which he'd first
become aware of when unpacking his books. Had the poet been
in less of a delirium when he'd taken on the tenancy, he might
have noticed the agent's undue haste in leaving the rooms. What
price a commission? The agent didn't like to think of the unfortunate legacy attached to the upstairs suite or was it simply a coincidence that anyone who roomed there subsequently met an
uncanny death within two years of leaving the property. As he
entered Johnson's name in the ledger, the agent supposed that
the 'short-stay' kind were not of the most stable variety.

Lionel Johnson's 'Dark Angel' was at hand: 'Thou art the
whisper in the gloom, The hinting tone, the haunting laugh:
Thou art the adorner of my tomb, The minstrel of mine epitaph'. A malevolent entity had long been associated with the
chambers that can only be described as a large shadow winged
creature with fearsome claws. The apartment was spacious and
secluded but as Lionel would confide to Ralph D. Blumenfeld,
the News Editor of the *Daily Mail*, there was something not
quite right about it. As a courtesy to the poet, Blumenfeld kept
Lionel's name out of his report: 'My friend filled-up most of the
wall space with books, read, wrote and mused during most of
the day and part of the night, and he admitted to me in his more
confidential moments that "things happened" there. He did not
specify exactly what had occurred, but after a time he became
nervous and fidgety.'

Lionel was still a tenant of Lincoln's Inn when Ernest Dowson died of tuberculosis on February 23rd, 1900, at the age

of thirty-three. The Rhymer's Club was no more. On February 28th, the day after Dowson was laid to rest in the Catholic section of Ladywell Cemetery, Lionel wrote 'Ash Wednesday,' dedicated to his friend: 'The visible vehement earth remains to me; The visionary quiet land holds thee: But what shall separate such friends as we?' Lionel Johnson, the rainy day man of letters, moved out of Lincoln's Inn as hastily as his ill-starred predecessors. His new dwellings, at Clifford's Inn on Fetter's Lane, was a stone's throw from The Cheshire Cheese where the Rhymers had once gathered.

Confined to his bed for much of the time, Lionel didn't bother to unpack his beloved books and they lay in their boxes gathering dust, like the letters that piled up in the hall, unread and unanswered. Though his family offered to pay a man to come in and assist Johnson, he declined, just as he declined medical intervention. The only outside help Lionel accepted was that of Annie Jenkins, a laundress who had attended to him since 'The Fitzroy Settlement' and popped in to cook a meal now and again. At the inquest, Jenkins would stress, that even at his lowest, Johnson possessed 'Beautiful manners.'

Of course, Jenkin's comment gave no light as to the poet's baleful condition but even in dilapidation he was noble. For over a year, Lionel Johnson barely stirred and received no social calls. But what of Lionel's friends? Following the death of Oscar Wilde on November, 30th, 1900, Lord Alfred Douglas sought reinvention. Never has a man reincarnated himself more in one life-time than Bosie. Whilst Johnson lay on his sick bed, the cash-strapped Douglas attempted to net a wealthy American wife, earning a rep as a gigolo, at least to his enemies who were legion and blamed him for ruining Wilde, but no relationship is ever that simple. Lionel had given a rave review to Bosie's second book of poetry, *The City of The Soul,* but sonnets do not a living make.

W.B. Yeats meanwhile was embroiled in Celtic phantasmagoria and may have missed the news story that ran in *The Daily Mail* on Thursday, May 16th, 1901, under the headline 'A London Ghost – Inexplicable Happenings in Old Chambers...' When Lionel Johnson vacated the Lincoln's Inn premises, he contacted Ralph D. Blumenfeld, explaining that 'He could stand it no longer.'

Blumenfeld, a reporter of some repute, decided to investigate the poet's allegations and rented the chambers for twenty-four hours, between May 11th and 12th. Blumenfeld was assisted by Max Pemberton, the editor of *Cassell's Magazine* and a member of 'Our Society,' a literary fraternity specialising in criminology that also boasted Arthur Conan Doyle amongst its associates. Having ordered the rooms to be cleared of all contents, aside from two chairs and a table, the two men went through the chambers as midnight approached, checking that they were completely empty, making sure that there were no secret panels or recesses where a person might have hidden themselves.

Satisfied, they sprinkled chalk dust on the polished floor and settled down to their vigil: 'The doors leading to the little rooms were closed and we sat in the big room and waited. We were both very wide-awake, entirely calm, self-possessed and sober, expectant and receptive, but in no way excited or nervous.' When the story subsequently broke, Johnson was not mentioned by name, Blumenfeld referring to the poet only as a 'Rather well-known man of letters' who had left the premises suddenly.

The first occurrence may just have been a case of heightened nerves when the door handle on the far right of the main room gave an audible click. Had the one on the left not done so in rapid succession, they may have concluded the old house was draughty: 'We talked again, but there was a tension, a restraint which we had not felt before. I cannot explain it, but it was there. Longish silences ensued, but I am sure we were both wide-awake. At 1.32 the right-hand door opened again, exactly as before. The latch clicked, the brass handle turned, and slowly the door swung back to its full width. There was no jar or recoil when it became fully open. The opening process lasted about eleven seconds. At 1.37 the left hand door opened as before and both doors stood wide.' For the next hour, the doors opened and closed at least four times, by themselves.

It was then that the men noticed claw prints in the chalk dust: 'There were three toes and a spur behind. The footprints converged diagonally towards the doors to the big room. And each one was clearly and sharply defined, with no blurring of outline or drag of any sort.' The article raised a great deal of interest and prompted a flood of letters to *The Daily Mail* along with calls for the Society of Psychical Research to commence a formal investigation. Mr E.T Bennett, secretary of the society informed the *Mail*:

> 'This particular story seems to be told with sincerity, and in a common sense manner that is unusual in such cases. Therefore it becomes really interesting. One of the objects of the society is to carefully inquire into alleged phenomena apparently inexplicable by known laws of nature and commonly referred by Spiritualists to the agency of extra-human intelligence. This seems to me to be such a case and I shall certainly bring it before the members of the society.'

In September 1902, Lionel Johnson rallied ever so slightly and found the strength to go through his correspondence. A letter written by Johnson to Lewis Hind, the editor of *The Academy*, is imbued with pathos, like a tiny flame flickering in a gale:

> 'You last wrote to me, some-time, I think in the last century, and I hadn't the grace to answer. But I was in the middle of serious illness, which lasted more than a year, during the whole of which I was not in the open air for even five minutes, and hopelessly crippled in hands and feet. After that long spell of enforced idleness I feel greedy for work.'

Hungry though he might have been for the intellectual sustenance that writing offered, Lionel wasn't strong enough to make good on his ambitions: 'Go from me, I am one of those, who fall' the epitaph already composed. A ghost in life, Lionel Johnson was a half-finished sketch of where the skyline meets the sea. Iain Fletcher, in the best summary of the poet's work, comments: 'The void that separates us from each other, that is Johnson's theme.' His gift was in composing the intangible and like his most atmospheric work, Lionel Johnson was comprised of haunted gossamer.

At thirty-five and besieged by disorder and poor health, Lionel Johnson was unable to take even the most hesitant steps back to a semblance of life. The prognosis, a blurring of paralysis, alcoholism and a series of strokes were mentioned at the inquest and in a series of written accounts. Richard Le Gallienne believed that the poet had been knocked askance by a hansom cab whilst author Henry Nevinson noted that he'd taken a tumble on the corner of Fleet Street. A porter from Clifford's Inn reported picking the poet up when he found him unconscious on the street outside. At the Green Dragon on Fleet Street, Irish poet Katherine Tynan commented that Johnson had fallen from a bar stool. The incident was raised at the inquest, where the barman testified: 'He came in looking very ill. He went to sit in a chair and in trying to do so he fell slightly on his head.' For a more robust person, the episode would have passed without note but Johnson was extremely fragile and the fall may have fractured his skull. The poet was taken, unconscious, to St Bartholomew's Hospital. In the early hours of October 4th, 1902, Lionel was given Extreme Unction by a Father Dawson – so uncannily close to Dowson – and the dedication he bestowed to Johnson in a poem of the same name; 'Yet when the walls of flesh grow weak, In such an hour, it may well be, Through mist and darkness, light will break, And each anointed sense will see.' ('Extreme Unction')

The rooms at Clifford's Inn were emptied with undue haste and little care, sheaves of poems are believed to have gone missing, the consequence of an unsympathetic landlord on the heels of Johnson's relatives. Of all the obituaries that carried testimony to Johnson's poetic gift, only *The Daily Mail* revisited the occurrence at Lincoln's Inn, identifying Lionel for the first time: 'Not the least strange fact in connection with this story is that Mr Johnson was at one time the occupier of the haunted rooms... it was stated to the inquirers who visited these rooms that previous occupants had died within a short period of leaving the rooms...'

The chambers at 8 New Square claimed at least two more victims, Robert Percival, who was murdered in the Strand and in 1913, Charles Appleby, a young barrister, perished after witnesses claimed they saw him fighting off a large shadow winged creature. Sad-eyed Lionel is said to haunt the area, at least according to a lawyer known as Shannon who practiced in Lincoln's Inn.

Ralph Blumenfeld, the author of the 1901 *Daily Mail* report, was always unwilling to say anything more. In the 1960s, the story was revived by Wentworth Day and Tony Parker. Parker said that Blumenfeld had told him that the house would be impossible to find, as it had been 'pulled down after the First World War and another building erected on its site.' Perhaps Blumenfeld was still trying to protect the identity and reputation of his old friend Lionel Johnson, and Parker did not catch on. Blumenfeld reassured him that there had been no haunting in the new building.

But the fact is that 8 New Square still stands, while no further sighting of the winged and clawed entity have been reported. The story of the 'Bird of Lincoln's Inn' carries a spectral resonance that appealed to none other than the Reverend of the Supernatural, Montague Summers. In his volume of memoirs, *The Galanty Show*, Summers recalled the case, being particularly sympathetic to Lionel Johnson... whose frail spectre he believed had been seen in the area.

Although W.B. Yeats barely acknowledged Johnson's death at the time, with the passing of the years, the void that Lionel left became more noticeable. Now W.B. Yeats knew what it was to be haunted: 'Perhaps his spirit, if it can care for or see old friends now, will accept this apology for an absence that has troubled me.' Lord Alfred Douglas remained enigmatic but when asked of his late friend, always remembered him with the greatest fondness.

Nina Antonia at the time-worn grave of Lord Alfred Douglas, the Franciscan Priory, Crawley. The grave stone is so badly eroded most of the lettering is illegible. Under no circumstances does it suggest that this is the final resting place of someone once of note.

WITHOUT WHOM 'DANCING WITH SALOME' WOULD STILL BE A WALLFLOWER OF THE IMAGINATION:

Therese Taylor

John D. Stratford

Caspar Wintermans

Darcy Sullivan

Vanessa Heron

Ken Summers

Clint Marsh

Beth Hall

Carl Abrahamsson

Vanessa Sinclair

Eli John

CRITICALLY ACCLAIMED
BOOKS BY NINA ANTONIA:

- *Incurable* (Strange Attractor Press)
- *The Greenwood Faun* (Egaeus Press)
- *The Prettiest Star* (Kindle Only)
- *Johnny Thunders – In Cold Blood* (Jungle Books)
- *The New York Dolls – Too Much Too Soon* (Omnibus Press/ Music Sales)

She has also contributed to a variety of publications including the only Fantasy/Horror publisher in Ireland, Swan River Press, *Wormwood*, a journal of decadent obscurity and wonder as well as *Fiddler's Green* who issued one of her Wilde tales as an esoteric comic, as well as a gamut of music magazines and some Rockumentaries such as 'Looking For Johnny' & 'Arthur Kane New York Doll.'

To find out more about Nina, don't go to Wiki where a numb-skull gave her a career as a singer rather than an author – instead go to www.ninaantoniaauthor.com

ALSO AVAILABLE FROM TRAPART BOOKS

Genesis Breyer P-Orridge: Sacred Intent – Conversations with Carl Abrahamsson 1986-2019

Sacred Intent gathers conversations between artist Genesis Breyer P-Orridge (1950-2020) and longtime friend and collaborator, the Swedish author Carl Abrahamsson. From the first 1986 fanzine interview about current projects, over philosophical insights, magical workings, international travels, art theory and gender revolutions, to 2019's thoughts on life and death in the the shadow of battling leukaemia, *Sacred Intent* is a unique journey in which the art of conversation blooms.

With (in)famous projects like C.O.U.M. Transmissions, Throbbing Gristle, Psychic TV, Thee Temple Ov Psychick Youth (TOPY) and Pandrogeny, Breyer P-Orridge has consistently thwarted preconceived ideas and transformed disciplines such as performance art, music, collage, poetry and social criticism; always cutting up the building blocks to dismantle control structures and authority. But underneath the socially conscious and pathologically rebellious spirit, there has always been a devout respect for a holistic, spiritual, magical worldview – one of "sacred intent."

Sacred Intent is a must read for anyone interested in contemporary art, deconstructed identity, gender evolution, and magical philosophy. The book not only celebrates an intimate friendship, but also the work and ideas of an artist who never ceased to amaze and provoke. Also included are photographic portraits of Breyer P-Orridge taken by Carl Abrahamsson, transcripts of key lectures, and an interview with partner Jacqueline "Lady Jaye" Breyer P-Orridge from 2004. This expanded edition also contains material written by Abrahamsson after Breyer P-Orridge's death in March, 2020.

Carl Abrahamsson: Temporarily Eternal – Photographs of Genesis P-Orridge 1986-2018

A photobook with snapshots as well as structured portraits of artist Genesis P-Orridge from 1986 to 2018. A great visual companion to P-Orridge's and Abrahamsson's highly lauded anthology of interviews, *Sacred Intent*, this book is an inspiring journey through the mind and life of someone who never stopped exploring and changing. Also contains an essay by Abrahamsson on P-Orridge's "psychic anarcho-sartorialism."

Genesis Breyer P-Orridge: Brion Gysin – His Name Was Master

Brion Gysin (1916–86) has been an incredibly influential artist and iconoclast: his development of the "cut-up" technique with William S. Burroughs has inspired generations of writers, artists and musicians. Gysin was also a skilled networker and revered expat: together with his friend Paul Bowles, he more or less constructed the post-beatnik romanticism for life and magic in Morocco, and was also a protagonist in an international gay culture with inspirational reaches in both America and Europe. Not surprisingly, Gysin has become something of a cult figure.

One of the artists he inspired is Genesis Breyer P-Orridge, who collaborated with both Gysin and Burroughs in the 1970s, during his work with Throbbing Gristle and C.O.U.M. Transmissions. The interviews made by P-Orridge have since become part of a New Wave/Industrial mythos. This volume presents them in their entirety alongside three texts on Gysin by P-Orridge, plus an introduction. This book is an exclusive insight into the mind of a man P-Orridge describes as "a kind of Leonardo da Vinci of the last century," and a fantastic complement to existing biographies and monographs.

Ruby Ray: Kalifornia Kool (Photographs 1976-1982)

Spanning music, art and literature, the industrial and punk scenes of San Francisco in the late 1970s and early 1980s were diverse but united by a DIY, anti-authoritarian attitude. Photographer Ruby Ray was there to capture it all in the same spirit. With her work appearing in the legendary punk zine *Search & Destroy* and its successor *RE/Search*, Ray was at the epicenter of, and a key participant in, a vital cultural moment vibrant with provocation and creativity. A local experimental music and art scene supported artists like Bruce Conner and William S. Burroughs, and attracted groundbreaking bands like Devo, the Mutants, Boyd Rice and the Dead Kennedys, as well as established international bands like Throbbing Gristle, the Clash and the Sex Pistols. *Ruby Ray: Kalifornia Kool* collects the photographer's images from this time: live shots, backstage parties, apartments overflowing with youthful exuberance, elegant portraits of key people and photographic experiments. Her work captures a time and a place where West Coast open-mindedness, youth, art, music and electricity merged.

"Late 70s, early 80s... Ruby Ray and her camera, capturing the movers and shakers of the San Francisco punk and industrial scenes... And then some... Performance art, music, literature, photos, videos made with a "fuck you" and "do it yourself" attitude. Ruby sees and Ruby captures... Knowns and unknowns, winners and losers, sane and insane, constructive and destructive... William Burroughs with his gun, Bruce Conner being fueled by punk energy, Sex Pistols' last ever gig in San Fran, Throbbing Gristle, The Cramps live at Napa Mental Hospital, Search and Destroy Magazine, and bands and gigs galore... Devo, Mutants, Slits, Bags, Dead Kennedys, Cabaret Voltaire, Roky Erickson, Nico, DOA, Chrome, Factrix, Boyd Rice, Z'EV, Flipper... You name'em and there was Ruby Ray: the spectacularly talented lens of Kalifornia Kool. We should be grateful for her work. It's invaluable, evocative, loud, sexy and more inspiring now than ever before... Ruby's images open up a portal to a mythic and frenzied scene and show that it's true: all mythologies are real... Turn up the volume and dive into this one." – Carl Abrahamsson, from the Introduction

Carl Abrahamsson: Different People

Different People is an anthology of interviews by Swedish author Carl Abrahamsson, focusing on art, life and the creative process. Included are in-depth conversations with Conrad Rooks, Malcolm McLaren, Stelarc, John Duncan, Charles Gatewood, Mark McCloud, Ralph Metzner, Peter Beard, Bill Landis, Ralph Gibson, Maja Elliott, Michael Bowen, Bob Colacello, Dian Hanson, Anton Corbijn, June Newton, Kendell Geers, Simeon Coxe III (Silver Apples), Vicki Bennett (People Like Us), and Brian Williams (Lustmord). These groundbreaking artists, writers, musicians, photographers, filmmakers, editors and psychedelic researchers have all helped shape the culture we live in. But what makes them do what they do? Which are their driving forces and their inspirations; their joys and fears?

Carl Abrahamsson: Fanzinera Expanded – Photographs 1985-1988

Swedish writer Carl Abrahamsson started taking photos to go along with the interviews he made for the fanzines *Lollipop* and *Acts Of Interstellar Torture* (1985-1988). From this vast and snap-happy collection comes *FanzinEra*... A selection which includes portraits and live shots of underground superstars like: Iggy Pop, Sonic Youth, Lydia Lunch, Richard Kern, Nick Zedd, Joe Coleman, The Gun Club, The Cramps, Union Carbide Productions, The Leather Nun, Screamin' Jay Hawkins, Alex Chilton, The Church, The Go-Betweens, Long Ryders, Died Pretty, The Scientists, The Saints, Sort Sol, Sator, John Lydon, Legendary Stardust Cowboy, New Order, The Godfathers, Genesis P-Orridge, Henry Rollins, Pere Ubu, Hüsker Dü, The Shamen, The Jesus and Mary Chain, Zodiac Mindwarp and the Love Reaction, Dom Dummaste, The Stomachmouths, The Nomads, The Creeps, Pushtwangers, Livingstones, Wylde Mammoths, Blue For Two and Cortex... To mention but a few! Also included are textual flashbacks and quotes from the interviews, full color reproductions of the fanzine covers, and an introduction by American photographer Richard Kern.

The Fenris Wolf 10 (2020)

Carl Abrahamsson – Editor's Introduction, Carl Abrahamsson – Onwards to the Source!, Ludwig Klages – On the Essence of Ecstasy, David Beth – Katabasis and Erotognosis, Henrik Dahl – An Introduction to Eroto-Psychedelic Art, Peter Sjöstedt-H – Antichrist Psychonaut: Nietzsche's Psychoactive Drugs, Carl Abrahamsson – Lux Per Nox – The Fenris Wolf As Libidinal Liberator, Jesse Bransford & Max Razdow – Revisiting the Veil of Dreams, Christopher Webster – Beyond the North Wind, Kendell Geers – A Long Boundless Systematized..., Kadmus – Seeking the Three-Headed Saint, Billie Steigerwald – The Chthonic Seed: Reflections of an Ancient Death Gnosis, Fred Andersson – The Gospel According to the Tomb Man, Zaheer Gulamhusein – Sunflower, Charlotte Rodgers – The Riderless Horse..., Craig Slee – The Occult Nature of Cripkult, Damien Patrick Williams – Daoism, Buddhism and Machine Consciousness, Philip H. Farber – Thoughts on the Creation of Memetic Entities, Thomas Bey William Bailey – Memetic Magick, Mitch Horowitz – Is Your Mind a Technology for Utopia?, Ramsey Dukes – I'm Gonna Blow Your Mind, Carl Abrahamsson – Grasping Reality with Gary Lachman, Anders Lundgren – Mike Mignola and the Lovecraft Circle, Peggy Nadramia – So It Was Written, Peggy Nadramia – Addendum to So It Was Written, Nina Antonia – Maya, Jack Stevenson – Häxan/Witchcraft Through the Ages, Andrea Kundry – The Demonic Cultural Legacy of Antonin Artaud, Joan Pope – The Birth of Ideas, Genesis Breyer P-Orridge – Idiosyncratic Use Ov Language..., Vanessa Sinclair – Try To Altar Everything, Claire-Madeline Corso – Cutting Up a New Conversation

The Fenris Wolf 9 (2017)

Vanessa Sinclair & Carl Abrahamsson – Editors' Introduction: Looking back at the crossroads, Katelan Foisy – Invocation: Homage to the spirits of the land/London, Sharron Kraus – Art as Alchemy, Demetrius Lacroix – The Seven Layers of the Vodou Soul, Graham Duff – Sublime Fragments: The Art of John Balance, Ken Henson – The American Occult Revival In My Work, Gary Lachman – Was Freud Afraid of the Occult?, Peter Grey – Fly the Light, Val Denham – Proclaim Present Time Over, Katelan Foisy & Vanessa Sinclair – The Cut In Creation, Claire-Madeline Culkin – Beds, Bodies and Other Books of Common Prayer – A Reading of the, Photography of Nan Goldin, Steven Reisner – On the Dance of the Occult and Unconscious in Freud, Katy Bohinc – The 12th House: Art and the Unconscious, Olga Cox Cameron – When Shall We 3 Meet Again? Psychoanalysis, Art and the Occult: A Clandestine Convergence, Ingo Lambrecht – Wairua: Following shamanic contours in psychoanalytic therapy at a Maori Mental Health Service in New Zealand, Elliott Edge – An Occult Reading of PAO! Imagining in the Dark with Our Vestigial Shamanism in a Shade, Shadow, Wide, Charlotte Rodgers – Stripped to the Core: Animistic Art Action and Magickal Revelation, Alkistis Dimech – Dynamics of the

Occulted Body, Fred Yee – Cut-Up As Egregore, Oracle and Flirtation Device, Robert Ansell – Androgyny, Biology and Latent Memory in the Work of Austin Osman Spare, Ray O Neill – Double, Double, Toil and Trouble: Psychoanalysis Burn and Surrealism Bubble, Derek M Elmore – Dreams and the Neither-Neither, Julio Mendes Rodrigo – Rebis, the Double Being, Eve Watson – Bowie's Non-Human Effect: Alien/Alienation in The Man Who Fell to Earth (1976) and The Hunger (1983), Carl Abrahamsson – Formulating the Desired: Some similarities between ritual magic and the psychoanalytic process

The Fenris Wolf 8 (2016)

Carl Abrahamsson – Editor's Introduction, Vanessa Sinclair – Polymorphous Perversity and Pandrogeny, Charles Stansfield Jones (Frater Achad) – Alchymia, Tim O'Neill: Black Lodge/White Lodge, Nina Antonia – Bosie & The Beast, Aki Cederberg – Festivals of Spring, Michael Moynihan – Friedrich Hielscher's Vision of the Real Powers, Friedrich Hielscher – The Real Powers, Orryelle Defenestrate Bascule – Ear Horn: Shamanic Perspectives and Multi-Sensory Inversion, Zbigniew Lagos – The Figure of the Polish Magician: Czesław Czynski (1858-1932), Gary Lachman – Rejected Knowledge: A Look At Our Other Way of Knowing, Carl Abrahamsson – Intuition as a State of Grace, Bishop T Omphalos – The Golden Thread: Soteriological Aspects of the Gnostic Catholicism in E.G.C., Kendell Geers – iMagus, Johan Nilsson – Defending Paper Gods: Aleister Crowley and the Reception of Daoism in Early 20th Century Esotericism, Gordan Djurdjevic – The Birth of the New Aeon: Magick and Mysticism of Thelema from the Perspective of Postmodern A/Theology, Tim O'Neill – The Derleth Error, Antti P Balk – Greek Mysteries, Carl Abrahamsson – The Economy of Magic, Stephen Sennitt – The Book of the Sentient Night: 23 Nails, Henrik Dahl – We Ate the Acid: A Note on Psychedelic Imagery, Jason Louv – Robert Anton Wilson's Cosmic Trigger and the Psychedelic Interstellar Future we need, Carey Hodges & Chad Hensley – New Orleans Voodoo: An Oddity Unto Itself, Alexander Nym – Kabbalah references in contemporary culture, Zaheer Gulamhusein – Standing in Line, Carl Abrahamsson – As the Wolf Lies Down to Rest, Vanessa Sinclair & Ingo Lambrecht – Ritual and Psychoanalytical Spaces as Transitional, featuring Sangoma Trance States, Hagen von Julien – Listening to the Voice of Silence: A Contemporary Perspective on the Fraternities Saturni, Erik Davis – Infectious Hoax: Robert Anton Wilson reads H.P. Lovecraft, N – II. Land, Cadmus – Neo-Chthonia, Kadmus – A Fragment of Heart: A contribution to the Mega-Golem, Stojan Nikolic – The One True Church of the Dark Age of Scientism, Miguel Marques – The Labors of Seeing: A Journey Through the Works of Peter Whitehead, Renata Wieczorek – The Conception of Number According to Aleister Crowley, Orryelle Defenestrate Bascule – Fragments of Fact, Derek Seagrief – Conscious ExIt, Kasper Opstrup – By This, That: A spin on Lea Porsager's Spin, and Genesis Breyer P-Orridge – Greyhounds of the future.

The Fenris Wolf 7 (2014)

Carl Abrahamsson – Editor's Introduction, Sara George & Carl Abrahamsson – Fernand Khnopff, Symbolist, Sasha Chaitow – Making the Invisible Visible, Vanessa Sinclair – Psychoanalysis and Dada, Kendell Geers – Tu Marcellus Eris, Stephen Sennitt – Fallen Worlds, Without Shadows, Antony Hequet – Slam Poetry: The Warrior Poet, Antony Hequet – Slam Poetry: The Rebel Poet, Genesis Breyer P-Orridge – Alien Lightning Meat Machine, Genesis Breyer P-Orridge – This Is A Nice Planet, Patrick Lundborg – Psychedelic Philosophy, Henrik Dahl – Visionary Design, Philip Farber – Higher Magick, Kendell Geers – Painting My Will, Carl Abrahamsson – The Imaginative Libido, Angela Edwards – The Sacred Whore, Vera Nikolich – The Women of the Aeon, Jason Louv – Wilhelm Reich, Kasper Opstrup – To Make It Happen, Peter Grey – A Manifesto of Apocalyptic Witchcraft, Timothy O'Neill – The Gospel of Cosmic Terror, Stephen Sennitt – Sentient Absence, Carl Abrahamsson – Anton LaVey, Magical Innovator, Alexander Nym – Magicians: Evolutionary Agents or Regressive Twats?, Antti P Balk – Thelema, Kjetil Fjell – The Vindication of Thelema, Derek Seagrief – Exploring Past Lives, Sandy Robertson – The Fictional Aleister Crowley, Adam Rostoker – Whence Came the Stranger?, Emory Cranston – A Preface to the Scented Garden, Manon Hedenborg-White – Erotic Submission to the Divine, Carl Abrahamsson – What Remains for the Future?, Frater Achad – Living In the Sunlight, Genesis Breyer P-Orridge – Magick Squares and Future Beats

The Fenris Wolf 6 (2013)

Carl Abrahamsson – Editor's Introduction, Frater Achad – A Litany of Ra, Kendell Geers – Tripping over Darwin's Hangover, Vera Nikolich – Eastern Connections, Carl Abrahamsson – Babalon, Freya Aswynn – On the Influence of Odin, Marita – Runic Magic through the Odinic Dialectic, Aki Cederberg – Afterword: The River of Story, Shri Gurudev Mahendranath – The Londinium Temple Strain, Gary Dickinson – An Orient Pearl, Derek Seagrief – Aleister Crowley's Birth & Death Horoscopes, Tim O'Neill – Shades of Void, Nema – Magickal Healing, Nema – A Greater Feast, Philip Farber – Sacred Smoke, Robert Taylor – Death & the Psychedelic Experience, Michael Horowitz – LSD: the Antidote to Everything, Alexander Nym – Transcendence as an Operative Category, Carl Abrahamsson – Approaching the Approaching, Renata Wieczorek – The Secret Book of the Tatra Mountains, Sasha Chaitow – Legends of the Fall Retold, Sara George & Carl Abrahamsson – Sulamith Wülfing, Robert C Morgan – Hans Bellmer, Genesis Breyer P-Orridge – Tagged for Life, Carl Abrahamsson – Go Forth and Let Your Brain-halves Procreate, Anders Lundgren – Satanic Cinema is Alive and Well, Anton LaVey – Appendices

The Fenris Wolf 5 (2012)

Carl Abrahamsson – Editor's Introduction, Jason Louv – The Freedom of Imagination Act, Patrick Lundborg – Such Stuff as Dreams are Made of, Gary Lachman – Secret Societies and the Modern World, Tim O'Neill – The War of the Owl and the Pelican, Dianus del Bosco Sacro – The Great Rite, Philip H Farber – Entities in the Brain, Aki Cederberg – At the Well of Initiation, Renata, Wieczorek – The Magical Life of Derek Jarman, Genesis Breyer P-Orridge – A Dark Room of Desire, Genesis Breyer P-Orridge – Kreeme Horne, Ezra Pound – Translator's Postscript, Stephen Ellis – Poems for The Fenris Wolf, Hiram Corso – Mel Lyman, Mel Lyman – Plea for Courage, Gary Dickinson – The Daughter of Astrology, Robert Podgurski – Sigils and Extra Dimensionality, Frater Nigris – Liber Al As-if, Peter Grey – The Abbey Must be Built, Vera Mladenovska Nikolich – A Different Perspective of the Undead, Kevin Slaughter – The Great Satan, Lionel Snell – The Art of Evil, Phenex Apollonius – The Quintessence of Daimonic Ipseity, Phanes Apollonius – Infernal Diabolism in Theory and Practice, Anonymous – Falling with Love: Embracing the Infernal Host, Lana Krieg – Sympathy with the Devil: Faust's Infernal Formula, Carl Abrahamsson – State of the Art: Birthpangs of a Mega-Golem, Carl Abrahamsson – Hounded by the Dogs of Reason

The Fenris Wolf 4 (2011)

Carl Abrahamsson – The whys of yesterday are the why-nots of today, Hermann Hesse – The Execution, Fredrik Söderberg – Black and White Meditations 1-23, Peter Gilmore – Every Man and Woman Is a Star, Peter Grey – Barbarians at the Gates, John Duncan – Hallelujah, Ramsey Dukes – Democracy Is Dying of AIDS, Tim O'Neill – The Technology of Civilization X, Thomas Karlsson – Religion and Science, David Beth – Bloodsongs, Payam Nabarz – Liber Astrum, Hiram Corso – Unveiling the Mysteries of the Process Church, Jean-Pierre Turmel – The Pantheon of Genesis Breyer P-Orridge, Kendell Geers – The Penis Might Ier Than Thes Word, Z'EV – The Calls, Robert Taylor – Dreamachine: The Alchemy of Light, Phil Farber – An Interview with Terence McKenna, Phil Farber – McKenna, Ramachandran and the Orgy, Thomas Bey William Bailey – The Twilight of Psychedelic America?, Ernst Jünger – LSD Again/Nochmals LSD, Baba Rampuri – The Edge of Indian Spirituality, Aki Cederberg – In Search of Magic Mirrors, Carl Abrahamsson – Thelema and Politics, Carl Abrahamsson – Someone's Messing with the Big Picture, Carl Abrahamsson – An Art of High Intent?, Carl Abrahamsson – A Conversation with Kenneth Anger

The Fenris Wolf 1-3 (1989-1993/2011)

Carl Abrahamsson – Editor's Introduction
Carl Abrahamsson – 'Zine und Zeit (2011)

The Fenris Wolf 1 (1989)
John Alexander – The Strange Phenomena of the Dream, Helgi Pjeturss – The Nature of Sleep and Dreams, Tim O'Neill – A Dark Storm Rising, Carl Abrahamsson – Inauguration of Kenneth Anger, Carl Abrahamsson – An Interview with Genesis P-Orridge, William S Burroughs – Points of Distinction between Sedative and Consciousness-Expanding Drugs, Carl Abrahamsson – Jayne Mansfield: Satanist, TOPYUS – Television Magick, Anton LaVey – Evangelists vs The New God

The Fenris Wolf 2 (1990)
Lionel Snell – The Satan Game, Carl Abrahamsson – In Defence of Satanism, Anton LaVey – The Horns of Dilemma, Genesis P-Orridge – Beyond thee Valley ov Acid, Phauss – Photographs, Jack Stevenson – 15 Voices from God, Jack Stevenson – 18 Fatal Arguments, Tim O'Neill – Art On the Edge of Life, Terence Sellers – To Achieve Death, Stein Jarving – Choice and Process, Tim O'Neill – Under the Sign of Gemini, 93/696 – The Forgotten Ones In Magick, Tim O'Neill – The Mechanics of Maya, Coyote 12 – The Thin Line, Genesis P-Orridge – Thee Only Language Is Light, Jack Stevenson – Porno on Film, Carl Abrahamsson – An Interview with Kenneth Anger

The Fenris Wolf 3 (1993)
Jack Stevenson – Vandals, Vikings and Nazis, von Hausswolff & Elggren – Inauguration of two new Kingdoms, Tim O'Neill – A Flame in the Holy Mountain, Frater Tigris – A Preliminary Vision, Carl Abrahamsson – The Demonic Glamour of Cinema, William Heidrick – Some Crowley Sources, Peter H Gilmore – The Rite of Ragnarök, ONA – The Left-Handed Path, Zbigniew Karkowski – The Method Is Science..., Fetish 23 – Demonic Poetry, Ben Kadosh – Lucifer-Hiram, Freya Aswynn – The Northern Magical Tradition, Anton LaVey – Tests, Austin Osman Spare – Anathema of Zos, Rodney Orpheus – Thelemic Morality, Nemo – Recognizing Pseudo-Satanism, Philip Marsh – Pythagoras, Plato and the Hellenes, Terence Sellers – A Few Acid Writings, Hymenæus Beta – Harry Smith 1923-1991, Andrew M McKenzie – Outofinto, Beatrice Eggers – Nature: Now, Then and Never

Carl Abrahamsson: The Devil's Footprint

God proposes the challenge of the millennium: if Satan sorts out the ever growing human mess on Earth, God will lovingly take him back to Heaven as his favorite Archangel. Satan accepts, and sets out on a massive operation to balance out over-population, pollution, corruption, and other severely Satanic headaches – many of which he originally helped create... Easier said than done! Satan's love of the ambitiously mischievous humans is challenged as his own "Team Apocalypse" fervently sets to work. But as the world begins to change quickly and dramatically for the better, a new question arises: can God and his suspicious Archangels really be trusted in this cataclysmic, cosmic undertaking?

Carl Abrahamsson: Mother, Have A Safe Trip

Unearthed plans and designs stemming from radical inventor Nikola Tesla could solve the world's energy problems. These plans suddenly generate a vortex of interest from various powers. Thrown into this maelstrom of international intrigue is Victor Ritterstadt – a soul searching magician with a mysterious and troubled past. From Berlin, over Macedonia, and all the way to Nepal, Ritterstadt sets out on an outer as well as inner quest. Espionage, love, UFOs, magic, telepathy, conspiracies, LSD, and more in this shocking story of a world about to be changed forever...

"It's a thrilling roller coaster ride through psychedelic adventures, juicy romantic interludes, metaphoric dreamscapes, high Himalayan yoga enclaves, telepathic portals, 60's flashbacks, magical constructs, secret government pursuits and many more twists that kept all three of my eyes open. It's a story that you'll definitely want to keep non-stop reading, which I enthusiastically recommend."
– George Douvris, Links by George

"Mother, Have A Safe Trip is a highly entertaining and thought-provoking novel. Chock-full of psychedelia, the book is also a much welcome addition to the far too few fictional works published dealing with psychedelic culture."
– Henrik Dahl, Psychedelic Press

"The dialogues are great. But it's too short. I wanted more."
– Genesis Breyer P-Orridge, Artist

"It's a wonderful read. A lovely book."
– June Newton/Alice Springs, Photographer

Carl Abrahamsson (Ed.): The Mega Golem: A Womanual For All Times and Spaces

An anthology of texts and images constituting the current Corpus of the Mega Golem – the talismanic being/sentience created by Carl Abrahamsson in 2009. With contributions by Carl Abrahamsson, Vanessa Sinclair, Kadmus, Gabriel McCaughry, and others.

Vanessa Sinclair: The Pathways of the Heart

Vanessa Sinclair's new collection of poems and collages is rooted in the dark earth of death, but to an equal degree it also celebrates the vibrant life-force that grows inside this eternal darkness, and the transformation, love and magic we all need to live. The constant interplay of motion and emotion filters fragments of questions we try so hard to avoid but always fail to. The Pathways to the Heart are many but they need to be trodden lightly, with love and deep appreciation.

Once there, you can assemble the fragments of your life and see what they say – the poetry of an existence that is inevitable until it is not.

Vanessa Sinclair: Switching Mirrors

Switching Mirrors is an amazing collection of cut-ups and mind-expanding poetry by Vanessa Sinclair. Delving into the unconscious and actively utilising the "third mind" as developed by William S Burroughs and Brion Gysin, Sinclair roams through suggestive vistas of magic, witchcraft, dreams, psychoanalysis, sex and sexuality (and more). Causal apprehensions are disrupted by a flow of impressions that open up the mind of the reader. What's behind language and our use of it? What happens when random factors and the unconscious are given free reign in poetic form? *Switching Mirrors* is what happens.

Vanessa Sinclair (ed.): Rendering Unconscious – Psychoanalytic Perspectives, Politics & Poetry

In times of crisis, one needs to stop and ask, "How did we get here?" Our contemporary chaos is the result of a society built upon pervasive systems of oppression, discrimination and violence that run deeper and reach further than most understand or care to realize. These draconian systems have been fundamental to many aspects of our lives, and we seem to have gradually allowed them more power. However, our foundation is not solid; it is fractured and collapsing – if we allow that. We need to start applying new models of interpretation and analysis to the deep-rooted problems at hand.

Rendering Unconscious brings together international scholars, psychoanalysts, psychologists, philosophers, researchers, writers and poets; reflecting on current events, politics, the state of mental health care, the arts, literature, mythology, and the cultural climate; thoughtfully evaluating this moment of crisis, its implications, wide-ranging effects, and the social structures that have brought us to this point of urgency.

Hate speech, Internet stalking, virtual violence, the horde mentality of the alt-right, systematic racism, the psychology of rioting, the theater of violence, fake news, the power of disability, erotic transference and counter-transference, the economics of libido, Eros and the death drive, fascist narratives, psychoanalytic formation as resistance, surrealism and sexuality, traversing genders, and colonial counterviolence are but a few of the topics addressed in this thought-provoking and inspiring volume.

Contributions by Vanessa Sinclair, Gavriel Reisner, Alison Annunziata, Kendalle Aubra, Gerald Sand, Tanya White-Davis & Anu Kotay, Luce deLire, Jason Haaf, Simon Critchley & Brad Evans, Marc Strauss, Chiara Bottici, Manya Steinkoler, Emma Lieber, Damien Patrick Williams, Shara Hardeson, Jill Gentile, Angelo Villa, Gabriela Costardi, Jamieson Webster, Sergio Benvenuto, Craig Slee, Álvaro D. Moreira, David Lichtenstein, Julie Fotheringham, John Dall'aglio,

Matthew Oyer, Jessica Datema, Olga Cox Cameron, Katie Ebbitt, Juliana Portilho, Trevor Pederson, Elisabeth Punzi & Per-Magnus Johansson, Meredith Friedson, Steven Reisner, Léa Silveira, Patrick Scanlon, Júlio Mendes Rodrigo, Daniel Deweese, Julie Futrell, Gregory J. Stevens, Benjamin Y. Fong, Katy Bohinc, Wayne Wapeemukwa, Patricia Gherovici & Cassandra Seltman, Marie Brown, Buffy Cain, Claire-Madeline Culkin, Andrew Daul, Germ Lynn, Adel Souto, and paul aster stone-tsao.

Sir Edward Bulwer Lytton: Vril – The Power of the Coming Race

Sir Edward Bulwer Lytton's cautionary tale of occult super-powers and advanced subterranean cultures have fascinated readers since 1871. Part early science-fiction, part educational tract, part occult romance, Vril keeps spellbinding readers thanks to its wide range of themes and emotions, as well as its thrilling sense of adventure.

A curious man descends into a mountain through a mine and experiences far more than he bargained for. Deep inside the mountain lies a completely different world. Its inhabitants, the Vril-ya, are human-like but physically superior and philosophically more advanced. They live in harmony made possible by their wisdom but also by the powerful and potentially destructive magical energy they call "Vril."

The impressed yet terrified visitor is allowed to stay and learn more about their ancient and advanced culture, something very few visitors have – it seems that all the previous adventurers have been mercilessly disposed of by the Vril-ya...

This edition includes an introductory essay by Swedish author Carl Abrahamsson.

More information can be found at our web site:

www.trapart.net

CPSIA information can be obtained
at www.ICGtesting.com
Printed in the USA
LVHW040115200422
716639LV00009B/1950

9 789198 692006